PRACTICAL SOCIAL WORK

Series Editor: Jo Campling

BASW

Social work is at an important stage in its development. All professions must be responsive to changing social and economic conditions if they are to meet the needs of those they serve. This series focuses on sound practice and the specific contribution which social workers can make to the well-being of our society in the 1980s.

The British Association of Social Workers has always been conscious of its role in setting guidelines for practice and in seeking to raise professional standards. The conception of the Practical Social Work series arose from a survey of BASW members to discover where they, the practitioners in social work, felt there was the most need for new literature. The response was overwhelming and enthusiastic, and the result is a carefully planned, coherent series of books. The emphasis is firmly on practice, set in a theoretical framework. The books will inform, stimulate and promote discussion, thus adding to the further development of skills and high professional standards. All the authors are practitioners and teachers of social work, representing a wide variety of experience.

JO CAMPLING

PRACTICAL SOCIAL WORK
Series Editor: Jo Campling

EDITORIAL ADVISORY BOARD

Terry Bamford, Malcolm Payne, Peter Riches,
Sue Walrond-Skinner

Working in Teams

Malcolm Payne

M

First published 1982 by
THE MACMILLAN PRESS LTD
London and Basingstoke
Companies and representatives throughout the world

ISBN 0 333 30886 7 (hard cover)
ISBN 0 333 30887 5 (paper cover)

Typeset by Cambrian Typesetters,
Farnborough, Hants
Printed in Hong Kong

FOR MARY

Contents

Preface

This book was written in 1980 when I was a lecturer in social work at the University of Bristol, and it draws on my own experience of working in teams and teaching about it, some of the literature on teamwork and the experiences of many others who have given me case examples and information; in particular, Renee Daines and Nick Welch provided the more extended case studies given in Chapter 7, Mary Marshall and John Cypher provided various contacts and my colleagues at Bristol University have given me useful examples of team-work in various ways. I am most grateful to them all.

I wrote the book on study leave. My thanks are due to the University of Bristol for giving me leave, Phyllida Parsloe for arranging it and giving her permission and support, and to my colleagues and friends on the CASS and PQRC courses who took up most of the extra work involved: Christopher Beedell, Roger Clough, Renee Daines, Philip Kingston, Pat Taylor and Sue Walrond-Skinner. Jan Bowyer and Nan Barker provided the secretarial support; Jan in particular took on some of my work and also arranged the typing of the main draft. Various of my placement and personal students put up with a transfer of tutor in mid-year to allow me to write the book; I am grateful and I hope they think the result was worth it. Jo Campling was a staunch supporter throughout, and her editorial skills and the help of Phyllida Parsloe and Renee Daines who have read parts of the text have improved it immeasurably. Mary Payne prepared the index and helped in all the other ways (Simon and Stuart, too). I appreciate very much all this kindness, support and help. Bristol University's School of Applied Social Studies was a fine place to work on teamwork and to have learned so much over the years.

Liverpool Council for Voluntary Service   Malcolm Payne
January 1981

List of Figures and Tables

Figures

Tables

Introduction

Structure

This book is written to help people in the personal social services understand teams and work in them. The first two chapters, containing about a quarter of the text, are mainly theoretical. They discuss various debates about the nature of teams and policy issues which arise around the use of teams in the social services. I have tried to draw attention to a wide range of literature on teamwork and to present a fairly unified perspective on different views, as a jumping-off point for the rest of the book. The terminology and analyses of different kinds of team are applied later on in the rest of the book. This is not, however, a full survey of the literature, because in order to meet my brief of providing a practical text I have avoided giving extensive details or academic justifications for every point. I have tried to explain the importance of the issues discussed, to make Chapters 1 and 2 integral to the more practical remainder of the book.

Chapters 3–7 are intended to provide a practical guide to ways of improving how a team works, dealing with problems which may arise within a team and, for individuals, working out their own relationships with their team. Although these chapters are mainly practical, they also point to relevant literature (e.g. in Chapter 6 on leadership and non-professionals, in Chapter 7 on multi-disciplinary teams). While the intention is to suggest ways of building teamwork skills — partly through referring the reader to books which contain exercises in team-building — the assumption behind most of this material is that it is best for teams to work out their own way of improving teamwork. I have tried to provide a variety of starting-points and systems to enable them to do so. There is consideration of a range of different types of team and issues in teamwork. I urge the reader to use the index to find references to the particular issue that your team wants to work on.

Chapter 8 discusses the practice of teamwork with clients in various ways and in a number of different settings. The discussion here is by no means exhaustive, but I have covered a number of difficult problems which often raise questions.

Assumptions

I have made a number of assumptions in writing this book. First, I do not think there is any one best way of working in a team. There are a number of good ways which suit different people in different situations in different ways. It may also be that no kind of teamwork is appropriate for you and your team. There are many disadvantages to teamwork in some situations. Thus, I am not concerned to promote teamwork everywhere and always.

Second, however, I take the position that the organisation of social services, the needs of clients and the community and the particular training and experience of many social workers suggest that collaborative teamwork may suit many social work situations admirably. This assumption, and arguments associated with it, appear throughout the book.

The third assumption is that there is a lot that can be said about teamwork, generally, and that can be applied to any form of team. Special roles and circumstances or particular needs are clearly indicated in some places by the sub-headings, but otherwise I think anyone could apply most of the points given here to any team. If the example given is not about your team, or I have given no specific application on a point which interests you, please stop and think how it can apply to your team. I cannot cover every situation, but I hope there is enough guidance here to help any social worker, indeed anyone in a team in the helping professions, work in teams a little more pleasantly and effectively.

Finally, a word about the tables of important points and analyses which appear at various points in the book. Although many of these could have been written into the text, I have produced them in this way to act as summaries and so that they can be easily found by looking at the list of figures and tables (p. x): I have suggested in several places that these might be worked on as check-lists, and it seemed useful to distinguish them in this way.

1

The Nature of Teams

Teamwork is in vogue in social work and in other helping services. Recent books on social work and recent government reports on the social services often recommend strengthening teamwork as a way of improving the organisation of services and the quality of the help given to the public. Many social workers assume that they work in teams and yet feel that their team is not as good as it might be. The biggest study of social services departments (SSDs), the United Kingdom's main social work agencies, found

> that no one interviewed in our field studies questioned the area team as the basic component in the organisation of the social services. Indeed, although it was seldom spelt out, our impression was that most social workers found it congenial to work in a team and relied, to a considerable extent, upon other team members for support. However, it was equally striking that social workers seem unaware of the potential of the team for team work (Parsloe, 1978, paras 14.73–14.74).

This book is a response to that liking for working in teams, and the opportunities for developing it. These opportunities rely on the assumption that the group is more than the sum of its parts: so, if you can get people to work together, they will create more than those same people working on their own could achieve. The question is how to organise working together so that it makes the best of the people involved.

Different kinds of team

This chapter is concerned with the problem of defining what a team is, and the first thing to note about that is the variety of different definitions. Debate about the nature of teams sometimes turns upon whether a team is really a team or whether it is really something else. The reason for such arguments is that the word 'team' denotes something that people are supposed to approve of. During a discussion of primary health care, Dingwall writes that the

> 'team' can be thought of as a device for concerting action. People can refer to 'the team' as a way of co-ordinating a set of individual activities. By implication, it seems plausible to suggest that the term came into use because it was felt that actions were not being concerted which ought to be (Dingwall, 1980, p. 114).

This suggests that the word 'team' may be used not only where a team (whatever it is) exists but also where someone hopes it does, or wishes it would. I am now going to try to make sense of the wide variety of meanings attached to the word 'team' and to make clear the ways in which I will use the term.

Most books or articles about teamwork are fairly clear that there is one sort of 'team' which is not really a team at all, and they are mostly severe in their criticisms about it. Such teams have been called 'traditional', 'undeveloped', or 'stereo-typed', but I prefer to call them *work groups* because this term is more neutral in tone. A work group exists when people are brought into relationships with one another by virtue of the fact that they work together; but they do not share work tasks or responsibility, and they do not use the fact that they work together to enhance the work that they are doing.

At the other end of the spectrum there is pretty clear agreement about the characteristics of what I call a *collaborative team*, and most writers are fairly friendly towards it. They use terms like 'fraternal', 'integrative', 'integrated', 'community', 'mature', 'idealist'. Here are some definitions of such teams:

Teams are collections of people who must rely on group

collaboration if each member is to experience the optimum
of success and goal achievement (Dyer, 1977, p. 4).

Teamwork is individuals working together to accomplish
more than they could alone (Woodcock, 1979, p. 3).

A team is a group of people, each of whom possesses particular expertise; each of whom is responsible for making
individual decisions; who together hold a common purpose;
who meet together to communicate, collaborate, and
consolidate knowledge, from which plans are made, actions
determined and future decisions influenced (Brill, 1976,
p. 22).

Ideally, teamwork involves the definition of common goals
and the development of a plan to which each member
makes a different but complementary contribution towards
the achievement of the team's aims (Hunt, 1979, p. 13).

A collaborative team, to put together the main elements of
these definitions, has common goals, and its members, while
they retain personal and individual responsibilities, divide up
their work so as to make the best of their activities and ensure
that they achieve those goals. Extending that definition to
apply it to teamwork (that is, what team members would
need to do in order to achieve such a pattern of work),
collaborative teamwork seems to require a process for deciding
on goals, a process for helping the members fit in their
personal skills and responsibilities, and a process for dividing
up and distributing the work. Teamwork has to be concerned
with the personal development of team members, with agency
goals, and with management. In spite of this agreement about
what is not a team and what is a very good team, there is a
lot of disagreement about all those 'teams' which do not fall
into either of these categories. How should they be defined
and, once defined, how regarded?

There are basically two approaches to this. One approach
is to say that teams change in a recognisable pattern: they
start as work groups when people first come together, and
they grow (if they are lucky or skilful) into collaborative
teams. This is called a *developmental* approach. Some people
argue that teams usually develop in this way, and this idea is

based on the assumption that teams have the characteristics of groups. There is some evidence which suggests that groups of people go through a common process of development, and Tuckman (1965) has reviewed the literature on this. He says that groups go through the processes of *forming* (getting together), *storming* (fighting over territory in the group), *norming* (coming to general agreement about how the group should work), and *performing* (getting on with work-sharing without worrying too much about relationships in the group). Brill (1976), whose book has been influential in social work, has taken up this approach and suggests that teams will go through similar processes of orientation, accommodation, negotiation and operation.

There are various shades of opinion about this developmental process. Brill tends to assume that if you put a group of people to work together they will usually work through these stages simply because group dynamics will always shift them in this way. Not everyone thinks this, however, because Woodcock (1979), although he uses much the same approach, says that many teams get stuck in an *undeveloped* (workgroup) stage, and have to be pushed to develop through stages of *experimenting* and *consolidating* (i.e. storming and norming) before they become collaborative (or *mature*, as he calls it).

This difference draws attention to a significant issue of definition: do teams develop through these phases, and, if so, what motivates or stimulates them to do so? Woodcock tends to the view that shifting to collaboration is so arduous that, human nature being what it is, most teams will need an outside push, and he is rather judgemental about those who have not responded. If you accept Brill's position, people, once put together, will tend to work better together naturally.

This leads me to the second approach to those teams which are neither collaborative nor work groups. This approach is perhaps best exemplified by Lewis (1975), who takes what I would call a *contingency* view. He says, in effect, that the type of team you have depends on the preferences of those involved, the nature of the work that they have to do, and the kind of organisation they are involved in. He concentrates on identifying the factors which distinguish between different team types, and leaves the middle group as an undifferentiated mass (which he calls 'federated' teams). This contingency approach leads to the position that many different kinds of team can coexist and be properly regarded as teams, and there is no suggestion that they necessarily need to be shifted along a continuum towards collaboration or that there is something wrong with the members if they refuse so to move. If you take a contingency view, you need to examine the people and their work to decide what kind of team they should have and what changes are needed to attain it.

As a compromise between these two approaches, it is possible to take the view that teams may or may not progress through stages, and if they do it will depend on the contingencies which affect them. Two examples of this approach are as follows. Lamberts and Riphagen (1975) describe their experience of working in a multi-disciplinary team in a health centre. They concentrate on how changes in various team members' perception of one another's roles caused (or was caused by) different views about goals and work relationships, and they imply that these changes derive from political interchange in the team around their different professional groupings. In my book about SSD area teams (Payne, 1979) I also took a compromise view, suggesting that the move from traditional through transitional to community teams arose when the team's relationship with the community it served and its pattern of services and staffing were changed.

To sum up this section on different types of team, I would suggest that teams can move through the kind of group development suggested by many writers, but they will only do so if the pressures which affect them make such a development relevant. Readers should be aware of one cautionary point. Ideas about team development rely rather heavily on the literature about groups, and although clearly teams are groups, most of the literature is concerned with therapeutic or experimental or growth groups, and the element in a work team of having specific tasks to perform in a wider organisation may mean that the literature is not directly applicable. The idea that a team can be treated as though it is just like any other group must be treated with extreme caution.

Second, I can mention at this point various other ideas

about defining teams in the middle range between work groups and collaborative teams which will be useful later. One is the work of Horwitz (1970), also discussed by Brill (1976). Horwitz says that there are identifiable *leader-centred* teams which are based on a person who controls team activity through charisma, the fact that team members are responsible to some superior through the leader, and the leader's personal and professional authority. Later, he mentions a *co-ordinative* team, which seems to include leader-centred teams where the leader is less dominant. My experience is that there are a lot of teams in the personal social services which cannot be regarded as work groups because they clearly share tasks and responsibilities, but are not collaborative because relationships are not equal. Horwitz's concentration on the role of the leader as a way of defining some teams seems a useful addition to the unmapped territory of the middle ground.

Another useful set of ideas is the taxonomy of teams presented by Webb and Hobdell (1980). (This taxonomy was previously published by Webb (1975), but the earlier paper is difficult to obtain.) They suggest that teamwork is intended to overcome the problems of specialisation by improving co-ordination, and to help specialisation by using the advantages of a division of labour. Specialisation is concerned with skills (the abilities of workers) and how they might be best *integrated* into a set of roles that a worker can sensibly carry out. The division of labour is concerned, on the other hand, with the tasks that have to be done, and *differentiating* them, or dividing them up, in a sensible way so that they can be given out to the different specialised workers. Tasks and skills can be heterogeneous or homogeneous, and Webb and Hobdell suggest that you can define different kinds of team according to how heterogeneous or homogeneous their tasks and skills are. Table 1.1 sets out their table (with amendments to provide clearer examples).

Finally, it is useful to distinguish *individualistic* teams from work groups. Many teams work in such a way that members operate independently, carrying out their own work in their own way, and this can be described as an individualistic pattern of work. It need not be regarded with the disapproval which is often attached to work groups, however, because

Table 1.1   *Taxonomy of teams*

Tasks (i.e. jobs the team must do)	Skills or roles (i.e. abilities of team members available to do jobs)	
	Homogeneous (members have similar abilities)	Heterogeneous (members have different abilities)
Homogeneous (jobs are rather similar)	*Collegial team* e.g. family practitioner team	*Apprenticeship team* e.g. social services team with different grades of staff
Heterogeneous (many varied jobs to be done)	*Specialised collegial team* e.g. SSD team with intake/ long-term or social care/ family-care specialisation	*Complex team* e.g. health centre team

(handwritten: skill mix)

Source: adapted from Webb and Hobdell (1980).

such individualistic work may reflect the needs of the client groups served by the team, the external pressures on the team and their own preferences. Even in teams where the work is carried out individually, there may be a considerable degree of joint planning to enable the specialist pattern to work, and responsibility may well be diffused among team members. Such teams may be involved in joint training or personal development even if their work is separate. All these factors create a category of team which is different from work groups.

It will be evident from the discussion so far that my own view of what a team is covers a fairly wide field. I think that if a group of people working together have shared goals, try to plan their work so that each individual's activities take account of that of others and attempt to use their togetherness to improve their work, then they should be regarded as a team. What characterises different types of team is the process by which they arrive at decisions about these matters, and in particular the structures set up to do so, their leadership and their external pressures and constraints.

Teams in the UK social services

Having looked at teams in general, it may be useful to examine some different kinds of teams which exist in the British social services. Two divisions can be made which overlap with one another. The *first* is into teams which are working mainly with individuals, families and groups of clients formed for the purpose of social work intervention (social work teams) and those which are responsible for work with naturally occurring groups in the community (community work teams). The *second* kind of division is into teams which exist in primary settings, where social work or social service is the main purpose of the agency, and those in secondary settings where social work is part of a set of activities whose main concern is other than social work.

) The social work team category and primary setting category include most of the major social service agencies in Britain: the area teams of social services departments, most teams in probation and after-care, most teams in residential and day centres of all kinds, and many teams in voluntary agencies if they are mainly concerned with services to clients. Such teams have certain advantages as settings for building up teamwork. The main purpose of the organisation (as well as the thrust of its activities) is social service, so expectations from outside the team should be more or less consistent with team members' wishes, or reasonably easily converted to those wishes. Moreover, social work teams and primary setting teams are dealing with a work group whose influential staff are social workers and others who are mainly ancillary to social work or of inferior status, so that inter-disciplinary and status issues are less difficult for the social workers (although others may find them hard). On the other hand, external constraints, such as those imposed by the courts on the probation and after-care setting, by local government on social services departments and by finance on voluntary agencies can seem more intractable because they cannot easily be dealt with inside the team.|

| The community work team, or a team with some community work component, and the secondary setting team present more difficulties for teamwork. The primary organisation may not share or understand their objectives; or the system

of organisation may not be appropriate. For example, Thomas and Warburton (1977) show in their study of community workers in a social services department that community workers used a different time scale for their work and had different objectives and values from other staff in the department, who made little attempt to understand or support their community work colleagues. Even in a community work agency, conflict with powerful groups in society over the values and objectives of the agency often arises. There is sometimes no clear dividing-line between the community work team and the public it works with — in which case, what is the team? Many of the same problems afflict residential and day-care workers in their isolation from the field-work orientation of many agencies and close involvement with their residents. Similarly, in day settings, social work teams have to work in an organisation where objectives may be in conflict or inconsistent with their aims. The status of a secondary activity may be in doubt and the completely different education and values of different groups of staff, particularly the primary group, may obstruct work. Education welfare officers in education departments, some housing welfare staff, and social workers in clinics and hospitals often face these issues. So, sometimes, do residential workers in homes whose main purpose is education, and day-care workers in centres whose main purpose is industrial production. The questions which arise for people in this position concern where the *boundary* of their team lies: should they maintain a separate identity in order to support their own values and goals, or should they merge with other groups to form multi-disciplinary groups? Often, they are seen as part of a looser network of workers (Hey, 1979) rather than a team. They are also faced with the question of their *domain*: What is the subject-matter with which they deal, and how can it, and the tasks and skills involved in it, be defined? And what are the meaning and implications of professional *status*, if your team represents only one of many different occupational groups? What are the implications for the *organisation* of managing work through teamwork? It is to these issues that the next chapter is addressed.

2

Some Implications of Teamwork

This chapter looks at some of the implications of encouraging teamwork in an organisation. Although many people tend to look on teamwork as an unreservedly good thing, it is equally possible to argue that individual creativeness and independence are as good or better, or to support competitiveness as the right form of organisation. So why should people in an organisation put themselves into teams, and what are the problems and issues which arise out of their doing so?

The team, the individual and the organisation

Teamwork is a way of fitting individuals into organisations, and the first group of issues and problems that teamwork raises has to do with this process. The obvious point is that teamwork, like any other form of organisation, is an instrument for carrying out the policy of the agency. Thus many management texts promote teamwork as a way of getting workers to do what the management of an organisation wants. Many social workers, however, tend to see teamwork as a form of mutual support, and might even see it as a way of influencing managers to do what they want, or as a way of preventing managers from having influence over them.

[An important issue for teamwork, then, is compliance, and it is raised in two rather different ways. First, does being in a team force an individual to comply with the wishes of the other members of the team, and thus limit their freedom of action? Second, does the fact that there are teams in the organisation make it more difficult for managers to get individuals to comply with their wishes? The answer in both cases is no; to understand why this is so, it is necessary to look at the kinds of power and influence which are normally used in social work agencies, and the evidence about how individuals comply with the normal forms of behaviour in groups.

French and Raven (1959) distinguish six different types of power: *reward*, where person A thinks powerful person B can reward him; *coercive*, where A thinks B can punish him; *referent*, where A identifies with B; *expert*, where A thinks B is more skilful or knows more than himself; and *legitimate*, where A accepts that a general view in society that B should be able to influence him is correct. To these Fraser (1978b) adds *informational* power, which arises when convincing information is available (but it is not limited to any one person), and this applies pressure to people to act in certain ways. This kind of power, obviously, is not possessed by any one individual, but is still a form of power influencing people's actions. Finally, it is important always to remember the point that particular patterns of power are inherent in the social patterns of our society, such as social class (Lukes, 1974).

Etzioni (1975) argues that a good way of understanding the differences between different kinds of organisations is by analysing the means used by managers to influence their subordinates. A review of research in his book suggests that therapeutic organisations (those concerned with helping others) tend to use less concrete forms of power which rely on symbolic rewards such as satisfaction, prestige, esteem and on making subordinates feel strongly and positively in the value of their organisation, so that they tend to support its aims. If you consider how vague the objects and methods of most social work agencies are, and how difficult it is to control how workers do their job, this approach to compliance is really the only one which has a chance of succeeding. So in a helping organisation a mutually supportive, sympathetic structure which helps workers feel involved in the planning of their work would be necessary. This is one way in which we can understand the resolution of the conflict between management and worker views of teamwork that I have identified.

But does involvement in teamwork force an individual to submerge their identity in the group? Many social workers feel that it does and are concerned about it, because they know of the extensive social-psychological research which shows that when you make decisions in a group people whose ideas are out of line with the rest tend to change their minds and conform, even when they are self-evidently correct and the majority wrong. There are three points to make about this.

First, as Fraser (1978b) shows when reviewing this evidence, recent research has shown that a committed minority can swing a majority, and this is particularly so when they can use informational power, and gain influence because they have a better knowledge of the problem. This tends to counter-act normative influence or group pressure. What may be happening in the traditional research is that the minority feel that the majority view is so manifestly absurd that they must know something unknown to the minority, and the minority lose commitment to their own view.

The second point is that independent views can have a very real influence on the whole group, even if they are relatively extreme; so creative views can have a chance in the group. How it works is complicated, but there is research into real-life decisions, including those made by clinical teams, where the views of the group as a whole took into account the views of each individual rather than polarising towards the majority.

The third point is that such changes often depend on the climate and attitudes in the group. For instance, if a group values taking risks, or being creative, and the way the group is run highlights that value, then groups actually appear in some research to support risk-taking and creativity (Fraser, 1978b). This is supported by some research into child-abuse case conferences in the UK social services (Perry, 1979).

In summary, then, it is quite reasonable to take the view that a team run in an appropriate way will not force anyone's compliance, but will permit a wide range of influences by managers and others; and that this pattern is relevant to the kind of work done in social work agencies and the patterns of power used by managers within them, so it can be argued that a team provides a good instrument in such a setting for managers to achieve the right kind of compliance.

A final point. Some people argue that creativity and flexibility are inherent in the openness and participative nature of a collaborative team, so unreasonable conformity is never an issue. But many teams are not of this type, and this statement applies only to conformity *within* the group. So individuals can on occasions feel constrained in groups and *external* pressure may be applied to the whole group. So I shall now turn to discuss how the whole team fits in with the wider organisation.

Team structure and organisation structure

There are three rather different ways in which you can understand the connections between a team (which is essentially a group) and the organisation within which it exists: hierarchical structures, systems ideas and matrix structures. |

Hierarchical structures

These structures assume that the teams are organised in a pattern so that some teams are more important than others and control the inferior teams, just as in line management, a superior sets the responsibilities of, and is in turn responsible for, his inferiors. Likert's (1961) link-pin idea is a well-known example. There are small hierarchies which form work groups each of which has a leader who is responsible for its contacts with other groups through his membership of the work group which surrounds his superior, who in turn is in a higher work group. This preserves the advantages of a hierarchy — clarity and certainty of responsibility — with the flexibility and commitment of teamwork. The problems of this system are threefold. First, the link-pin has to cope with membership of two groups which may be in conflict. Although this can be difficult, there is the advantage that link-pins are clear that the relationship between the teams is clear hierarchical authority. The second problem is that, if it is assumed that the link-pin is the leader, the structure tends to define the team's leader; and the particular person thus identified may be an inappropriate leader, either for that particular group as a whole, or for part of its activities. These issues are discussed further in Chapter 6. The third problem is that the link-pin is responsible for the work of the group in a simple hierarchical way, but a more collaborative team will tend to share that responsibility so that one person does not clearly retain it. Managers outside the team then feel that the team is out of control, or the leader is not properly in charge.

There are several points that can be made in reply to such criticism. First, a good collaborative team which is sharing responsibility will know who is responsible for what, so that responsibility is clearly held even if it is shared by several people. The role of the team leader then becomes to ensure that adequate clarity of definition exists. Second, critics should be clear that they are talking about responsibility and not blame. Very often in a complex matter the attempt to hold one person to blame is inappropriate, and the tendency of hierarchies to assume that this is possible is wrong.

Very often, large social work agencies have modified a hierarchical structure to form a link pin system, and something like it is common in SSDs. Figure 2.1 overleaf gives an example. Seven work groups and their link-pins are identified — in a full structure there are many more.

Systems ideas

The systems approach to understanding how teams fit into organisations tends to regard organisations as being made up of a variety of small groups. You can understand how they relate to one another by looking at influences between them. This means that if you are a manager you do not have to worry about what goes on inside the team. Neither do you need to define a leader as one who must be the one to fit in with the rest of the organisation. In effect you look at inputs and outputs. Information, instructions and pressures are fed into the team, which processes them, and you see results in the kind of work that it does. This can be monitored, and the pressures placed on the team altered accordingly. This allows

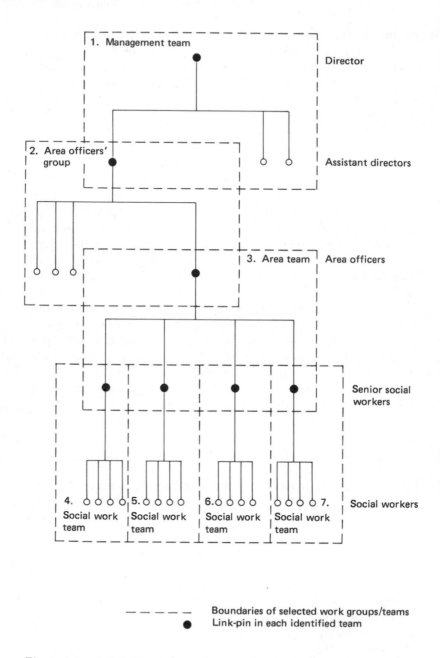

1. Management team
Director

2. Area officers' group
Assistant directors

3. Area team   Area officers

Senior social workers

4. Social work team
5. Social work team
6. Social work team
7. Social work team
Social workers

— — — — — Boundaries of selected work groups/teams
● Link-pin in each identified team

Figure 2.1 *A link-pin structure in part of a social services department*

the team freedom to organise itself in the way that it wants, and it is connected with the rest of the organisation through its outside contacts. No one part of the organisation is assumed to be in authority over another, though it may have ways of applying more pressure, or particular kinds of pressure, that are not available to all the other groups.

This is, however, a rather ideal description of what should happen; in practice two problems get in the way. First, there is the question of boundary. All systems have a boundary, and the definition of a boundary is that the amount of activity and exchange of information is greater inside the system than across the boundary (Anderson and Carter, 1974). What this means is that once a system is set up and working, it is sometimes difficult to influence it from outside. I am not talking here about influence on individuals by individuals, but about whether and how an outside group, like a group of managers, can act on a team as they would wish. The issue here, then, is inter-group relationships. If influence between groups is difficult, this will tend to lead to frustration and poor communication. There is some evidence that such difficulties exist in SSDs (DHSS, 1978) where teams are almost impervious to influence from other teams. Research into inter-group behaviour reviewed by Tajfel (1978) suggests that this may not always be a serious problem. He discounts the theory that strong groupings will always produce conflict because the group members feel a need both to belong and to fight outsiders. It is only where supposedly equal groups are treated by others unequally, or there is conflict for resources, or one group behaves in what others see as an unfair manner, that conflict arises. Avoiding such behaviour tends to reduce conflict between groups deriving from strong boundaries and team spirit.

(Another problem with the ideal systems view is that of group structure. The ideal view says that outsiders can exercise influence which fits the team into the organisation, and the whole team will be affected by it. But this assumes that the internal structure of the team permits the pressure to influence where it should, and it does not always work like this. Looking at how some group structures may work shows how it may go wrong.

Fraser (1978b) identified three forms of group structure which are usually important. *Affective* structures have to do with who likes whom. Generally mutual liking or disliking can be very powerful influences upon how the team works; neutral or mixed feelings about another team member are less important. *Communication* structures directly affect how a team works. The main issue, according to Shaw (1964), is the amount of centralisation in communication; it is centralised if one person controls a lot of communication, decentralised if communication is controlled by different people at different times and for different purposes. Centralised communication deals more quickly with simple problems; decentralised communication leads to fewer mistakes in complex problems. People tend to be happier with decentralised communication. If outsiders use inappropriate systems for the issue they are dealing with, or there are different assumptions about what the best system is, or the team is using an inappropriate system, communication and all activity will be hampered. *Power* structures are also important. I have already identified various different forms of power; if there are different assumptions between the team and outsiders about what kind of power can be used, and who has particular forms of power in the team, relationships between the team and others are hampered, and the whole organisation may run into difficulties. Other kinds of structure are *status*, and a lack of shared assumptions about who has or should have high or low status can affect relationships; the *flow of work*, which is concerned with how work should be passed between different parts of the organisation; and *roles* in the group.

Gostick's (1976) study of the work of an intake team provides an example of how the internal structures of a team may lead to apparently strange results. This team faced an increase in the amount of work, and it might have been expected that as a result they would have passed more work on to the associated long-term team. In fact, as work increased, more cases were closed and more work kept in the team rather than being passed on. I would suspect that this response occurred because of boundaries, and the associated differences in structures of work flow, status, power and communication.

If you do take a systems view of teams in an organisation,

therefore, it is important to bear in mind boundary and structural issues. Otherwise, it is easy to assume that teams as groups fit into an organisation rather more smoothly than usually is the case. |

Matrix structures

A matrix structure can resolve some of the problems of taking a hierarchical or systems view of how teams fit into organis- ations. In this case individuals are assumed to form part of a normal hierarchical structure or part of their normal groups within the organisation, but representatives are drawn from different parts of the structure or different groups to make up teams which work on particular tasks. They then have an allegiance both to the structure from which they originally came, and to the special team and its task. The matrix team can be managed by similarly representative teams drawn from higher levels in each relevant hierarchy. The arrangement may be temporary, for a specific piece of work, or a fairly permanent structure, designed to link different patterns of organisation. Figure 2.2 shows a simplified diagram of such a structure.

| A matrix structure is typical of the multi-disciplinary approach in the health service, where workers form a group in their own specialism but divide up to form clinical teams of different specialisms to serve groups of patients. In the Avon child guidance service, for instance, staff are drawn from the SSD (social workers), the education department (psychologists) and the health authority (psychiatrists and administrative staff). One each of these forms a matrix team serving an area, but each is part of its own specialised team in the separate departments. One senior official is drawn from each employing agency to manage the service (the matrix hierarchy) and individual members of staff have lines of accountability within their own organisation. |

| The problem with this kind of arrangement is that staff bear the whole burden of trying to reconcile the differences between the different organisations, and boundaries between different activities are more difficult to draw. But these are the very advantages of the scheme: different specialisms are

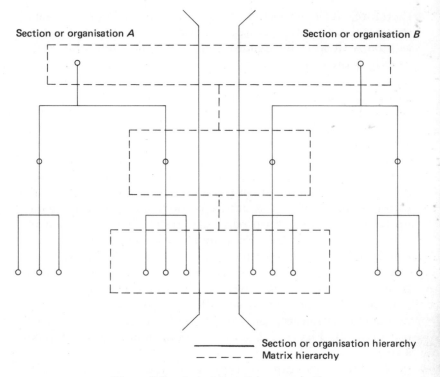

Section or organisation *A*

Section or organisation *B*

——————— Section or organisation hierarchy
— — — — — Matrix hierarchy

Figure 2.2 *A simple matrix organisation*

able to work together in an integrated activity; and there may
be advantages in blurring the distinction between different
forms of activity. The next section of this chapter therefore
moves on to look at how teamwork can affect the definition
of roles and tasks.

Role and task definition in teamwork

I have mentioned several times so far that good teamwork is
usually assumed to lead to better definition of activities
carried out in organisations. The simple reason for this is that
(theoretically) if a group of people are sharing a job of work
and all contributing to it, they naturally have to define clearly
what they are doing in relation to one another, otherwise the
organisation ends in chaos. This advantage is only theoretical,

however, because defining work activities is difficult to do at
the best of times, and is a controversial issue in social work,
and in many teams in social work it has proved difficult to
clarify matters sufficiently to permit good teamwork. The
more complicated reason why teamwork is assumed to be
bound up with task and role definition is that by some
definitions (e.g. that of Webb and Hobdell (1980) discussed
in Chapter 1) teamwork is concerned with differentiation and
integration of work. Lawrence and Lorsch (1967) suggest
that in order to deal with the external environment in which
they work, organisations have to split themselves into seg-
ments according to what is required of them (differentiation)
and then find ways of integrating these parts into a coherent
whole.

An important distinction to make is between tasks and
roles. Tasks are the components of jobs to be done, and are
defined by looking at a total workload and splitting it up
(differentiation) in a sensible pattern. Roles are the expectations that exist — defined by various different people — of
a particular worker, or the position in a team that he occupies.
Roles are usually constructed by knitting together a collection
of tasks which seem to go with one another reasonably well.

There are basically two ways of defining tasks, according
to Briggs (1973). *Job factoring* involves taking an area of
existing responsibility and dividing up tasks within it. Organisations often go about this in one of two ways. The 'droppings'
approach identifies high-level tasks which can be delegated,
and the 'bottoms-up' approach looks for all the jobs which
can be done at a lower level and passes up those which cannot. The good points about either of these approaches is that
they do not use new concepts, so they are easy to understand,
and they do not cut across existing definitions of skill and
status, so they do not stir up trouble. The problem with them
is that they are conservative and make it difficult to take a
completely different look at the activities of an organisation.
Developmental or *functional* approaches to task definition
start by identifying objectives for an agency, looking for
tasks which will meet them, and combining these into roles.
Because they start from an analysis of factors outside the
nature of tasks as they are currently defined (e.g. client need,

community need, the whole agency's need; see Teare, 1970) they can be more radical, and can respond to new policies and needs. They often run into difficulties because people cannot understand new definitions of tasks, or see how they can be put into practice, and by blurring existing roles they can run into professional or union resistance.

A number of modern analyses of social work tasks exist, most based on the work of Teare and McPheeters (1970) and Fine and Wiley (1971), both of which are functional analyses. British applications of their work, from BASW (1977) and Jeans (1978), are discussed in Chapter 4.

| Using task and associated role definitions can help to clarify who does what in a team, but they can lead to major policy issues which make teamwork a matter for controversy and debate. The reasons for this are summed up by Sheps (1974, p. 11):

> The examination of new roles in team development in the field of human services indicates that they do not spring from the logic of what one or two professions involved in a particular set of problems perceive. Instead, pressures built up by the demand for service which cannot be met by the traditional professions or traditional teams force the traditional profession or team to enlarge its member-ship. |

) Two important examples of what has happened, and the effect teamwork changes can have, lie in the development of para-professional work and multi-disciplinary teamwork in the health services. In both the USA and the United Kingdom much of the interest in teamwork has come from the growth of the use of non-professionals (i.e. paid ancillary staff such as social work assistants, called para-professionals, plus volunteers) and multi-disciplinary teamwork. Working with non-professionals tends to force teams to be less precious about so-called 'professional' skills and this leads to a more fundamental examination of their work. Multi-disciplinary work tends to have the same effect because professional workers are forced into contact with other disciplines of learning (e.g. psychology, sociology, medical science) and

come to see the limitations of their own discipline more
clearly.

Such changes also raise status issues, because it becomes
apparent that existing professional definitions of role are not
relevant in such a pattern of work. In the health service, therefore, social workers and nurses have seen teamwork as a way
of sharing decision-making with powerful professions such as
doctors. Teamwork can attack status definitions in this way,
but runs up against controversy because professional status
distinctions are based on much wider social differences. For
instance, the status of professions tends to be determined
along class lines, which are perpetuated because high-status
professions tend to recruit from the children of other high-
status professions (Pavalko, 1971). Another example is that
status in teams is often determined by gender. Women tend
not to achieve high-status positions in hierarchical team
structures, and women's professions (e.g. nursing) tend to
be of lower status than professions (e.g. law, medicine) where
men predominate.

Ideally teamwork could reduce such differentiation according to class and gender. But what often tends to happen is
that teamwork is used by higher-status professionals to reinforce their status. In surveys of non-professionals in the
USA, it has been shown that many non-professionals arc
fixed in lower-status jobs and do not get the chance to
progress. In the United Kingdom nearly all home helps and
most social work assistants are women, employed on low
wages, and rarely promoted. McIntosh and Dingwall (1978),
discussing doctors' attitudes to teamwork, suggest that
doctors may see the team as a way of reinforcing their
position in the health service, and maintaining, rather than
sharing, their control of decisions.

Advantages and limitations of teamwork

I now sum up the discussion in the first two chapters of this
book concerning the nature of teamwork and its usage, and I
hope that this will provide a basis for considering teamwork
practice in the remainder of the book.

In Chapter 1, {I considered a variety of different ways in which teams can be understood, and some types of team which can be distinguished. I took the view that the right kind of team for a particular group of people depends on the external pressures and what the team members' preferences are — you cannot say that one kind of teamwork is always the best. Collaborative (open and sharing) teams, work groups, leader-centred teams and individualistic teams are quite common in the social services. I pointed to two different approaches to how teams change and whether they progress: the developmental approach, which suggests that they usually go through a well-defined process of change and, given the chance, will usually end up as a collaborative team; and the contingency approach, which suggests that what happens will depend on the forces which affect the team. {

In Chapter 2, I have looked at a variety of issues which are debated in teamwork. I suggested that teams do not force individuals within them to comply with group norms, and that individuals can have their effect in teams even if they are in a minority. Similarly managers of teams do not have to worry that teams will get out of control and not respond to their influence — provided that the influence they seek to have is reasonable. I have discussed three ways of looking at how teams can link into the wider organisation of which they are a part — through hierarchical structures, through systems ideas and through matrix structures — and I stressed the importance of the limitations of each of these approaches and cautioned against an idealistic acceptance of any one of these. Finally, I pointed to the importance of task and role definition in teamwork, and to the consequences for how professions are seen and for conventional assumptions about status that implementing teamwork and changes in task and role definition may bring.

In summary, the possible advantages of teamwork are that it usually satisfies team members more than a competitive or controlling organisation, and this is important in helping professions where co-operation is particularly important and where there are no clear job definitions and distinctions. Teamwork can thus produce better work in the social services than other systems, it can make better use of human resources, and it can make work processes clearer and more explicit, for the benefit of both clients, social workers and managers.

On the other hand teamwork has its limitations. The organisational and work pressures on any particular team may obstruct the way in which teams work. The preferences of team members, and particularly its leader, may, if they are hostile, limit the applicability of teamwork. The boundaries created by teamwork, and difficulties in defining tasks and roles, together with commitment to various forms of status among team members, may limit the effectiveness of teams. Finally, team members may not be very good at using team structures to get work done. This is a limitation, however, that it *is* possible to overcome. Learning to work better as a team member may also make it easier to overcome the other problems outlined above. I hope that the remainder of this book will help in meeting some of the problems, by offering opportunities to improve your teamwork.

3

Assessing Teams and Work Groups

This chapter is about how to look at teams and work groups to find out how they work and how they might be changed. Team assessment is important to individuals thinking of joining a team who want to know what their future experience is going to be like, and to managers, whether inside or outside the team, who are thinking about trying to improve its teamwork. Some of the general principles are the same in either case.

Criteria for assessing teams

As a start, I think it is useful to try to identify what variables in team behaviour you might look at in order to see how a team will work. I have based these on a number of writers, but in particular an important article by Rubin and Beckhard (1972), Brill's (1976) functional yardstick for assessing teams and Woodcock's (1979) team building-blocks. In Chapter 1 I emphasised some of these points as important aspects of teamwork.

The first variable is clearly *goals* and how they are agreed, since I have argued that shared goals are an essential part of teamwork. Similarly the importance of external pressures and team members' preferences suggests that both *internal and external expectations* of the team are important variables. Another factor which I have emphasised before is how *leadership* is organised. Then, although I am cautious about regarding teams solely as the product of group dynamics, *communi-*

cation and group processes are important in describing how any team works. Related to that, and to shared goals, it is usually helpful to examine what shared *value systems and norms* exist among members of the team, since these will colour decisions about what is important in their work.\ Also, *how decisions are made* is an essential part of joint work in teams as opposed to individual work. These are the obvious points, but to them I would add two further variables and a caveat. One is the importance of *self-development and regular review of work,* since I shall try to show later in this book how important is thinking about others as individuals, and that teamwork cannot be maintained without regular arrangements for checking out how this is working. The final variable is the *physical environment.* This is often forgotten by theorists (but not by Barker and Briggs, 1969), but clearly the layout and facilities of an office or other setting for team-work can make or mar attempts at sharing. The general caveat is the importance of looking at these matters in relation to the needs of the clients and communities served by the team and the team's agency. A good example of doing this is Wood's (1978) article on probation team assessment. It is so easy to work out a method of teamwork which serves social workers rather than those they are supposed to serve.

Team assessment from the outside

Being on the outside makes it difficult for job-seekers to get a clear idea of how a team which they might join works, and direct questions may bring answers which are difficult to interpret. From the position of the outsider, the assessment variables indicate some of the things it is important to ask about. The individual's own preference is, of course, import-ant. There is no point in searching for collaborative teams if you prefer to get on with your own work individualistically, or if you feel that firm management by a charismatic leader is best for you. It is also unlikely that you will find an ideal collaborative team. Most are strung out along the continuum between work groups and collaborative teams, and individuals will have to seek those factors which are important to them.

Does the team have goals and how were they agreed? Generally speaking, a more collaborative team is likely to have a clearly defined set of goals, arrived at by an explicit exercise in mutual sharing but influenced by external pressures. Work groups will assume that goals are spelt out by managers or legislation. Leader-centred teams will rely on the leader to set the goals, with perhaps some prior discussion, especially about how to implement them.

What's your relationship with your boss? The important thing here is how *clear* relationships are. In a collaborative team everyone knows the kinds of things they can do for themselves or that they should go to the leader about. Answers like 'we get along pretty well' reveal a concern for easy rather than explicit relationships typical of a team towards the work-group end of the continuum.

What's the system for organising work? This is another way of getting at internal role expectations. Again, a collaborative team would have a clear system which involved a lot of participation and discussion in setting it up, though one person — often the leader — may administer it. Lack of system, or 'we sort things out as we go along', implies non-collaborative teamwork.

How does this team fit in with the department? A collaborative team would describe rather complex relationships in which the team can influence the agency, while the agency supports and influences the team. If it were suggested that there is not much mutual influence and contact between different parts of the organisation or that a simple hierarchy exists a less collaborative structure is implied where the possibilities of mutual influence are not perceived or used.

What style does the team leader have? Teams usually have leaders appointed. Some teams deny that there is a leader. This may mean an ideal collaborative structure, or that they are deluding themselves and are all dominated by some un-official leader. Collaborative groups recognise that leadership exists and they know how it works. Where there is an appointed leader, the more collaborative team has a leader who is seen as supportive but capable of being influenced by his team, who talks things over with the team as a group, who does not interfere when he has delegated authority, but who is very clear about the boundaries of his own authority. Many leaders are reasonably supportive, but only individually, and do not get involved in the group process as a means of doing their work. This tends to be the case in leader-centred teams.

How is a new policy that will be unpopular introduced? This is a good question to ascertain how the leader works. Teams at the work-group end of the continuum will tend to say things like 'you have to accept what the management wants sometimes'. In such teams even unpopular changes are introduced by administrative fiat. In collaborative teams unpopular things will have been openly discussed in the group because the team knows that the quickest way to break up is to ignore strong feelings about something. This is why Woodcock concentrates on co-operation *and conflict*, and openness *and confrontation* as essential building-blocks in teamwork. Both are required in a collaborative team.

How does the group work? It is almost impossible to get a clear answer to this, though a good collaborative team may be so well worked out that they can even describe this. At least there should be regular group meetings in a collaborative team and there should be a known and often-used structure for everyone, not just the leader, to raise issues there. If possible, an outsider wanting to find out about a team should attend a meeting. In a collaborative team all team members should make some contributions and no one should dominate. There will be signs of open disagreement and conflict, but they will not be personalised. If the leader seems to make most of the running and there is a formal air, the team may be tending towards a leader-centred style. If there is a lot of dispute which seems personally motivated, the team may be going through the accommodation stage of team development. While this is unpleasant at the time, it may lead to a more collaborative style, because it is a sign of change and future openness. As the team moves on in this way, openness is more accepting of individual differences, and disagreements are malice-free attempts to find answers to problems.

What do you disagree about at the moment? This is another way of seeing whether the collaborative value of dealing openly with conflict is accepted, or the non-collaborative style of repressing conflict.

Do you find you can support and trust each other? This ascertains the norms of a team. Most people in non-collaborative teams concentrate on their individual cases or jobs, and are allocated responsibility for all the work in a case. Collaborative teams, at the other end of the spectrum, will agree that more than one person can be involved in a few cases at an early stage and will describe joint projects. Another question which is relevant here is: *do you mind if someone else does something with one of your cases while you're out, or do you expect it to wait until your return?* Preference for the latter indicates a rather individualistic team. It is also worth looking at the use of non-professionals. It is quite common for parts of the work on a case to be delegated to them, or for them to have cases of their own. The sign of a collaborative team is where an enquirer is told that they are specially skilled at something or that they are involved in planning work in cases together with social workers, because this shows that lower-status workers are valued, and I have argued that this usually leads to more collaborative work.

Decision-making has already been covered in the discussion about goals so the next issue to be considered is the involvement in review and self-development.

What plans are there for promoting personal development? Is there any system for looking at how the team works? In collaborative teams these two issues will be seen as related. As I have argued elsewhere (Payne, 1981), the development of the team and of individuals within it are inseparable; both aspects affect each other. In non-collaborative teams planning will be worked out on the basis of individual needs rather than team needs, or at most the *leader* decides what is best for the team. In collaborative teams their programmes are devised after analysis and discussion by the group. There will also be regular reviews of team working and goals, whereas less collaborative teams will not see any value in such activities.

How does the layout of the office affect work patterns? There are two issues here which can be checked. One is *flow*. Does the layout make sense in relation to the movement of work between people? The other is *proximity*. Are people who need to work together close to one another, or are groups, e.g. manager and clerks, separated off? Sometimes access to individuals is very limited, e.g. by a closed door, or a routine which means that a team member is often unavailable to colleagues.

Team assessment for a manager

Many of the same kind of questions might be asked by a manager seeking to assess a team. Often, however, a manager will be concerned to see whether problems encountered with a work group are due to ineffective teamwork or to some other reason. The factors that Dyer (1977) proposes as relevant are as follows: *domination* by one person who prevents freedom of expression by others; *cliques and in-groups* which constantly dispute but never seem to resolve issues; *inequalities* in participation and use of resources among otherwise equal team members; *rigid* procedures or role capabilities in the team which no one is allowed to change; *climates* of defensiveness in dealing with colleagues or fear of their reactions to others; *uncreativeness* and lack of ideas for alternative ways of doing things when there is a problem to be solved; *communications* are restricted between some members of a work group; *conflicts*, whether actual or potential, are avoided rather than faced.

Team assessment by the team

While the idea of a team assessing its own functioning might be ideal, when members are used to the way things are they often find it difficult to see what could be changed and in what ways. Also, change is often promoted by individuals, and if dominant people in the group are satisfied with existing practices, others may not be able to start team assessment. This is why collaborative teams reason that regular open review is important, so that any problems will be raised and dealt with as a matter of routine. One way around this is to propose a *team review*, arguing that if no problems are found morale may be reinforced; and if problems do exist at least a start has been made on correcting them by finding them. Another way is to start from some proposed *change* as the basis for team assessment (e.g. when a new manager arrives, several team members arrive together, or a new project involving some members of the team begins). Any one of these can affect how the roles of all members are integrated and their skills differentiated, so a call for a review may be more acceptable at such a time. |

Attitudes in the team

One way of starting an assessment is to see whether people in the team feel that problems do exist. Some questionnaires are available for doing this (e.g. Woodcock, 1979, pp. 24–8; Dyer, 1977, pp. 36–8, 68–70), but there are two arguments against using such instruments. First, they tend to operate on the assumption that collaborative teamwork is the form which should be aimed for, and anything but this seems to be regarded as 'not-teamwork' and therefore to be denied rather than assessed. Second, I prefer to use a method of assessment which comes from the team itself; it should then be more suitable for their problems, and appropriate to their personal preferences.

A useful approach is to try to work out what kind of team exists, to see what satisfaction there is about the present state oi affairs, to find out what changes might be acceptable and then to plan moves towards the changes. A general discussion about whether the team is, say, collaborative or leader-centred would probably be inconclusive, so some kind of structure to such an exercise needs to be devised. For instance, different members of the team could be set up to investigate and argue that the team has the characteristics of each of the common team types that I have discussed: collaborative, leader-centred, individualistic, or work group. They can put up their arguments at a meeting and the team can assess the evidence for each. There are usually cases to be made in all teams for some characteristics of each being present. A useful rule in such debates is that a number of examples of actual behaviour must be listed in support of each argument — say, three examples. For instance, if the team member arguing that the team is mainly collaborative says that communication is open, the evidence might be that there was open discussion with the team before an unpopular directive from more senior management was implemented, that a social worker felt safe enough about her senior to dispute an important decision, and that an office procedure was actually changed after a team discussion even though it was a favourite procedure with the senior. To structure the debate, each of the assessment variables discussed earlier in this chapter could be dealt with in turn. As the debate reaches agreement on each variable it should prove possible to say that, in terms of each variable, the team is, say, leader-orientated or individualistic. Another variable may show something different; teams rarely come out the same on all variables. All members can make a note of whether they like the way the events used as evidence turned out, or how they would like to have seen it done differently. It is also worth comparing the evidence used for different team types to see if it comes from one part of the team's work. For example, if all the examples for the team being a work group come from, say, the office administration, while other aspects of the team's activities are more collaborative, the focus of future team change may have been identified, as may be the fact that work in the office is of a different and inconsistent nature with the rest of the team's activities, and that something should be done about it. As another example I have often come across teams where different client groups were served by different team patterns within the same group of workers. One team I have met is highly collaborative in its intermediate treatment work, individualistic in mental-health work, and leader-centred in child-care work.

Some people find the debate structure artificial and unhelpful because it highlights difficulties; others get confused by the arguments and are unable to come out with a clear result; still others find keeping strictly to the evidence rule is very difficult. A more co-operative structure for getting at the same ideas is to allocate various members of the team one or two of the assessment variables to research and to work together on their results. Again, the idea is to come up with a view about whether on each assessment variable the team is collaborative, a work group, leader-centred or individualistic — and then to judge whether that is desirable according to the team's preferences and the work they have to do and decide in what direction any change should occur.

I have purposely avoided being too specific, so far, about the particular judgements and evidence which would lead team members to come to one conclusion or another about their teams; I am not inviting an academic exercise in which the team's results have to be comparable with every other team's results. I merely seek to get people talking in a team about what their team is like and what it ought to be like, and I think it is better that people make their own judgements. This may be excessively unhelpful, however, so in the next paragraph I set out some of the main differences that I would expect to see between teams of different types on each criterion. Some words of advice about the kind of events which can be useful as evidence may be helpful. Teams might find it useful to look at things that they do not do, that they do not like. They could try to ask the opposite question for everything they say about themselves. If they get on well together, a useful question is to ask why they do not get on badly, because most groups of human beings get on badly at some time or other, and they may be suppressing conflict in order to cut down on strife. In suppressing conflict team members may be suppressing important aspects of relationships in the team. It can also be useful to look at totalities. If the team decides that it provides poor services for the elderly, are there some groups of the elderly that they do well for, or some part of their services which is good? No picture is ever unremittingly good or bad.

Finally, a few clues about the sort of evidence I would

expect to find about the style of team in the case of each variable. In a *collaborative team* I expect to find that there is an open and planned goal- and priorities-setting exercise in which all the team participates, that team members feel they are consulted about and influential in deciding on the sort of work that they do, that leadership passes around members of the team at various times for appropriate purposes, that people talk openly and without animosity about conflicts and problems, that many decisions are made jointly by more than one person (rather than by individuals), that team members often talk over and agree about personal and political ideologies, that decisions are usually discussed explicitly before action is taken, that the personal development of team members is attended to, and there is a regular review of team working and personal progress. In a *leader-centred team* I expect to see much the same pattern, but with leadership in most situations retained by one person, the leader playing a dominant part in all decisions which arise, and the repression of conflicts and problems. An *individualistic team* would have a rather different pattern. Goals, priorities and roles would derive mainly from individuals' decisions about what they were to do, with gaps and overlaps taken up by individuals as they were revealed. The leader would tend to be an adviser, consultant, channel of communication and supporter of individual initiatives. Action and ideals might well be shared explicitly, though there would be no attempt at uniformity. Groups would not be a medium for decision-making or action but be more for information-giving. *Work groups* would have explicit, planned goals, mainly set from outside the team by more senior managers. External expectations would usually set what roles the team members took on. The leader would be a channel of communication and authority, with the organisation the absolute arbiter of decisions. Communication would centre on the leader, group processes would be irrelevant or used to control the team, value systems and norms would be irrelevant, the leader would make decisions on behalf of the organisation, would delegate some at his/her discretion, and any review would be undertaken by the leader or from outside.

It may be useful to give an example of a team which cannot

be collaborative in nature because of its work and the agency it is part of. It also takes in several team types. In one hospital team there are five social workers, each of whom works in different clinical teams on different wards and specialities. They have social work team meetings to deal with general issues in their relationship with the hospital, and to present a united front on the approach they take to their work. They also provide mutual support on a fairly open and equal basis. It is impossible for them to share work and, as a social work team, it is necessarily individualistic in style.

Several of these social workers operate in very different kinds of clinical teams. One works mainly with people recovering from strokes in a multi-disciplinary group where there is much mutual discussion and no professional speciality dominates, working in pairs and groups of staff with individual patients (a collaborative team). Another works mainly with surgical cases in which work is shared in a ward round where each speciality in turn expresses its point of view and the consultant allocates work to each according to their speciality (leader-centred). They are all reasonably satisfied with the pattern of teamwork that they experience.

Particular aspects of work

An alternative way of assessing teamwork is to look at a particular problem or sector of work. In my experience many teams do it this way: it is easier to start by focusing on a problem rather than a team process — it is less daunting. Work on the problem then provides evidence for thinking about improving the process, and the team will also gain the experience of working together. Starting by working on a problem also emphasises the point that teamwork is for contributing to better work, not just for having a happier work group. Moving towards collaborative teamwork, however, means that at some point the team must work on process issues.

Problems which can particularly help to assess teamwork are setting work priorities, identifying a system for allocating work tasks and specialisations, finding a decision-making process for dealing with social policy or difficult treatment issues (e.g. something better than case conferences, or the present system for allocating old people to residential homes) and a staff development or training programme. Ways of working on these issues are considered in the next chapter.

Individual needs

The third way of assessing a team is to start from individual needs and build up to a team programme to develop those needs. The strategy is to hold a series of interviews with staff members to identify their personal needs for training and staff development. Alternatively, an exercise can be built up to assess needs either in general or in a specialised part of the agency's work. Self-positioning exercises are one example of such programmes which I have used successfully with student and staff groups (Payne, 1980, 1981). Many different activities for use in staff-assessment exercises are contained in Priestley *et al.* (1978), Brandes and Phillips (1979), and Woodcock (1979). If interviews are used, the interviewer need not be the team leader; instead members of the team could interview each other (not forgetting the team leader), and this has the advantages of cutting down the time needed and reducing the effects of his formal authority on the results.

Individual needs can then be listed by the team as a whole, and shared, over- and under-developed interests or gaps can be identified. Action can then be planned to deal with them.

What kind of action?

Having identified the problems or needs, the next stage is to decide what to do about them. This involves, first, deciding which of the alternatives might be possible, and second, seeing if that would suit team members.

The alternatives

The first option to be considered is to make no great change. This should be looked at seriously, partly because it allows people who are satisfied with their lot to stake their claims and say how far they will go. Also, changing the way groups of people work is a long and arduous business, and should not be embarked upon lightly.

The other end of the spectrum is a *team-building* exercise, in which attempts are made to push the team along the road to more collaborative working, and ideally towards collaborative teamwork. This should also be looked at with caution, because people in the team, especially the leader, may not find it a congenial way of working and because it may not fit into the organisation, being an extreme and difficult-to-attain pattern of work.

In the middle of the continuum the team may be able to agree on particular matters they would like to improve upon; in looking at the assessment variables the team may be able to identify such issues.

The preferences

Looking at the preferences of team members may involve looking again at the assessment variables one by one. Lewis (1975) argues that some fairly clear conditions need to be fulfilled before a team-building exercise moving towards collaborative work is worth while. He suggests that these include the kind of work the team does, but in addition teams might look to see whether the following factors apply to them (if so, a collaborative team could be useful): the fact that there is a good deal of interdependence between the team's work and that of others; rapid change in how the team's task is defined; flexibility in decision-making is needed; understanding the whole organisation and its activities is important for getting things done; a lot of consultation between specialists; frequent informal communication; rapid changes in the structure and work of the agency; the use of new, complicated or rapidly changing techniques; and rapid changes in external pressures are part of everyday working. I would argue that most of these conditions apply to most social work agencies. The other kind of conditions have to do with members' preferences: it is only worth establishing team-building if the leader prefers shared decision-making and if group members' attitudes and work patterns are potentially compatible.

Outside help or not?

The remaining question is whether a team needs outside help in getting on with changing its way of work. Much of the management literature which suggests this is necessary is written by people who make part of their living as consultants. My view is that an outside consultant is useful where team members and the team leader are inexperienced or frightened of dealing with group processes (*clue*: when people say things like 'but we don't know what's going to come out'). A consultant can also be useful when the team members are unhappy about speaking up, particularly if their leader is involved, where there is unresolved conflict or apathy in the team, or no experience in running group programmes or exercises, or where the team needs an injection of self-confidence. In these cases a training officer, a member of another team or agency, or a sympathetic lecturer from a local college, may be a suitable consultant.

On the other hand, if team members are carrying out a fairly limited exercise which is not directly concerned with group processes, leadership and communication problems, but instead with matters like priorities or specialisation, most social work teams should be able to manage, *provided* that there is a good deal of commitment among members to doing it.

Even so, sometimes group processes and relationships become more central than expected when an unexpected problem arises. Outside help (which is helpful, not because it is expert, but because it is from 'outside' and the consultant can say what he thinks and is less affected by group processes) can be called in then, and the issue can be dealt with as it arises or shelved for a later exercise. Most social workers like working on their own work relationships as well as their clients', so once started on improving teamwork, enjoyment and progress can easily overcome the occasional hair-raising moments.

4

Team Development

Different ways of team-building

This chapter concentrates on ways of developing teams as groups, and in the process considers problem-solving, task and role structures in general. Dealing with individual relationships is considered in Chapter 5, but people concerned with developing relationships in teams without wholesale team-building exercises will probably need to use some of the structures discussed here. Two alternative strategies are possible, one in which there is a direct and explicit concern with group *process*. Alternatively, the *content* of some process of working together can be altered: since an aspect of working together changes, so too do group processes.

The basic point of teamwork (of whatever kind) is working *together*, so any team-building programme must have *some* concern for group process. However, it may be better if team-building is concerned with content, rather than with work on group processes directly. There are various reasons for this, some actively for this view, and some against the process view. For the content view it can be said that it is easier to justify, inside and outside the team, activities which are obviously directed at the content of the agency's work; that they can have an immediate, often beneficial, effect on work; and that they are less daunting than individual relationships to start on. Process work, on the other hand, is exciting and interesting to many, but only indirectly affects the work of the agency. As Parsloe (1972) says of 'self-study' as a preparation for groupwork, it is really a different order of activity. It is also irritating and irrelevant to a few people, who, in a small work group, might disrupt things. Finally, direct work on group process needs a trained facilitator, who may be expensive and hard to come by, and only rather indirect benefits may be realised.

This chapter therefore concentrates on content ways of working.

Awareness of group processes

Teams do need to be aware of group processes, however, and such awareness can be promoted by easing and review.

Easing

Any group activity needs to be eased so that people feel open, comfortable and relaxed. This is useful either when tensions are raised in a sticky patch of discussion (to let off steam), or to start and finish proceedings. It is important to allow plenty of time for gossip, coffee, meals and activities outside any serious discussion as well as places for privacy, away from the atmosphere of the main programme. Discussions can be helped by an 'exercise' style (i.e. using a series of games or simple projects), rather than just 'talking'. This helps to balance serious and difficult matters with a 'fun' element and to set limits on particular activities, so that people do not expand the implications of their topics until everything loses focus. The exercise format of one subject at a time provides a focus without the need for heavy chairmanship.

Another useful idea is to have 'ice-breakers' and 'relaxers' at the beginning and end of each session. These should not take more than a few minutes, if that. They should be quite irrelevant, even silly, but require a certain amount of concentration and interaction. Children's games are often useful, e.g. Simon (or O'Grady) says, or exercises like putting everyone in a circle and getting them to sit on each other's laps. (Games like this which involve touching should only be used with groups which have had a good deal of social contact.) A number of suitable games are included in Brandes and Phillips (1979, I, 124—40). These activities release tensions, make people concentrate on things other than the problems of the session and help create togetherness.

Reviewing

¹After each session or set of activities, group processes can be reviewed. *General reviews* consist of a session in which people are invited to discuss how relationships in the team have changed, how they feel about them and what happened in the previous few sessions that gives evidence about team processes.¹ Evidence can usefully be about team structures, e.g. communication, power and influence, liking and alliances, and personal roles in the team. Such a discussion is difficult to manage: it may be helpful to maintain a spirit of enquiry by using what is known as an *enquiry mode* (see p. 50). For instance, in one probation team discussion at the end of a session on work priorities, a member said something like: 'I realised when we cut Ron off short, that we often do that when he talks about divorce court welfare. I know he's interested, but I think I'm a bit frightened of divorce. Perhaps we could talk about training for that or something.' In the event the team decided to have specialisation rather than train everyone in work not all of them wanted to do, but the comment is an almost ideal group process evaluation. It makes everyone realise that they were partially responsible as a group for making Ron bore everyone with his hobby-horse, rather than solely blaming Ron, it criticises no one, and it looks for a way of solving the problem.

Playing *rounds* is a less daunting method of review because the limits on self-expression are stronger. The best rounds for this purpose are 'I learned . . .' and 'I still need to learn . . .'. Everyone in turn is asked to say something about previous sessions in this way: no one else can comment, but all can gain from the insight of others. People can 'pass' if they want to. Crosby (1972, p. 15) has some useful rules for both these kinds of feedback: 'You will tend to be helpful when you are specific. You will tend to be judgmental and *not helpful* when you are general and evaluative' (emphasis original).

A third, more private, way is through *self-watch*. Here each team member is asked to make comments about activities under explicit heading (I often issue a batch of forms for each participant). There might be categories for knowledge, skills, feelings and attitudes learned both for the team member or about others, and open spaces for records of feelings or responses. It is useful if these are shared with another; often it helps to accumulate them for several sessions to see if there is a pattern. Then, individuals can help each other in pairs by sharing their perceptions, afterwards reporting back to the group on anything of general importance.

Content-based team-building

Having set up and agreed within the team ways of easing and reviewing group processes, the team can move on to think about how it organises its work. I do not discuss staff and team development as an approach to this, because I have considered it at length elsewhere (Payne, 1981). This leaves decision-making processes, task differentiation and role integration as the three approaches to be discussed here. They are dealt with in this order, because problem-solving structures may become relevant to all the others.

Team-building through problem-solving

Some teams are reasonably happy with how they get on together and how they organise their work, but find it hard to get new projects going, to represent their views and needs to outsiders, or to respond to issues which affect them as a group or as individuals. This may mean that their decision-making and problem-solving processes need improvement. Decision-making in the team is basic not only to projects and policies but also, on a smaller scale, in therapeutic activities which involve several people working together. Solving a problem in a team differs from individual problem-solving. For the solution to work, team members have to agree about and commit themselves to the problem and the solution, to

work together in order to get the desired results and co-
ordinate that action. Individual problem-solving is unaffected
by these things (which may be why some people prefer it).
On the other hand, team problem-solving has advantages
because it gives a broader constituency so the team can say
that there is wider support for their action, and the work
involved in a difficult task can be spread using different skills
that one person may not have.

The essence of team problem-solving is obtaining commitment and planning and co-ordinating action. At the planning
stage the team needs to know who will do what, when, where
and how, and how it will get feedback about what happens.
There may be problems if one or more of these points is
missed. An example of this is a case conference decision
about the discharge of a child from care. It was agreed that
the residential staff (who) would discuss the arrangements
(what) with parents and child (who) and fix a date (when).
The social worker (who) would pick up the parents, bring
them to the house and return them (what) with the child
(where), borrowing the agency's car for the purpose because
the worker's was too small for the luggage (how). As the
agreed date approached, the child became upset about going
home. When the parents and social worker arrived there was
an unpleasant scene. The parents were upset, and accused
the agency of turning the child against them. At the next case
conference the social worker accused residential staff of not
telling her what was going on and the residential staff said the
social worker did not care about the child's feelings, because
she had encouraged the parents to be demanding. Later, the
meeting came to the conclusion that the social worker's 'bad
handling' of the child had arisen from the poor communication about responses among parents and child when they
were told about arrangements. Each had treated it as the
other's responsibility to prepare *their* clients (social worker—
parents, residential workers—child) and fell back on 'I've
done my job — you haven't done yours' accusations when
adequate feedback between them would have allowed more
realistic preparation of both sides. Things might also have
gone better if they had discussed the bad side of the decision
with children and parents as well as the good side, and had

consulted the parents and child rather than just *explaining* what was happening.

ı This case illustrates the crucial importance of making explicit arrangements for feedback between the parties in team decision-making, even where things are expected to go well. In this case the tasks were differentiated, with clear responsibilities given to each, but their roles were not integrated properly. ı

If you keep in mind the aim of getting who, what, where, when, how and feedback clear, problem-solving has more focus. The next requirement is to obtain *commitment*. This involves making clear exactly what problem the team wishes to solve and what aim it wants to pursue in order to solve the problem. All aims imply problems, and all problems can lead to aims for overcoming them, but an objective may relate to a lot of different problems, and any one problem might lead to a number of different ways of doing things. This means it is vital to clarify *aims, problems* and the *relationships between them*, otherwise members of the team can become confused. For example, a team of education welfare officers (EWOs) thought that a group of schools was not referring enough children to child-guidance clinics, and set about trying to build contacts between the psychologist and head teachers. A number of misunderstandings followed, so they met to reconsider their project. They discovered that they had two rather different aims and several different problems. One aim was to strengthen the child-guidance service (and probably covertly to have more involvement *vis-à-vis* SSD social workers); another was to strengthen consultancy to teachers in the school. The problems were variously seen as an increase in delinquency among pupils, poor co-operation among professionals, poor handling by teachers of pupils in schools and unreasonable demands for advice from EWOs. Because different strategies were implied, depending on what a particular EWO thought was the problem, and different problems were mentioned to others involved, the head teachers and the psychologist were unclear what they were being encouraged to do.

Another important point is making sure *all the relevant factors* have been identified. A way of doing this is *brain-*

storming. A period allocated in a team meeting in which everybody makes as many suggestions as possible, no matter how silly, and they are all recorded. The important factors are that the period is short and everyone has to keep up the flow of ideas, there should be no selection so that everything is noted and, vitally, there is no evaluation at this stage. The different ideas are grouped and evaluated later. The aim is to get lots of ideas, not just good ones. From a joke suggestion, brilliant ideas can grow, because jokes often rely on incongruity – they imply a leap away from the ordinary.

The team must also obtain *agreement about the main problem or goal.* If there is conflict about this, the team can divide into small discussion groups. *Conflict and consensus groups* are sometimes useful. A conflict group contains people who disagree over a point and are set to find a solution to their conflict. These can work extremely hard and produce a workable compromise. A consensus group is a group of people who all agree that something is important but cannot think of ways to deal with it. They are set to produce recommendations for action. Curiously, in the process of analysing an issue, a consensus group sometimes breaks into furious argument because something they all agree about in vague principle raises all kinds of issues of detail which have been immobilising them from action. Itemising all these as a result of the consensus group's task to get practical action often clarifies a vague problem.

One difficulty is that people often tend to think in shorthand: they think about aims or solutions before, or at the same time as, the problem. An example of a common occurrence that I find in training social workers is as follows. I asked a group of experienced students to look at the case of an elderly lady and identify the problems she faced. The first three answers were solutions, not problems: 'she needs a home help', 'she needs a slot meter' and 'she needs a volunteer to visit her'. Their experience suggested the sort of thing which often works in this kind of case. But if a team is trying to find a way out of a difficult problem, suggesting solutions like this is less useful than analysing the problem, which can suggest new avenues for action. Experience, by its nature, can only suggest old ones which have probably already failed.

Analysing and *evaluating problems* and *proposals* for action is the next stage. In many cases it will be necessary to find out more information, so the first useful step can be to identify problems and solutions that need this approach and seek ways of obtaining the information. *Force-field analysis* is a useful way of analysing problems and possible solutions (Merry and Allerhand, 1977, pp. 169–72). It involves listing all the factors which are either pressing for a solution in one direction, or raising a problem, and factors which either work against that solution, or suggest that a particular issue is not a problem. These can be given a weight (1 = major, 5 = minor) so that the seriousness of positive or restraining forces can be identified. The idea comes from Kurt Lewin's field-theory. It is possible to construct diagrams to show the opposing forces; an example is given in Figure 4.1. It is easy to pick off or emphasise particular forces one by one in either direction, and to see the relative importance of immovable forces. Deciding what is really immovable will give the best clues in deciding the best approach. Each factor can be examined to see if it is as serious as team members think, if there are ways round it, or if there are opposing forces which counter-balance it. An accurate eye for opposition viewpoints is a useful skill. A Johari window (see p. 66) can also be used for problem-solving.

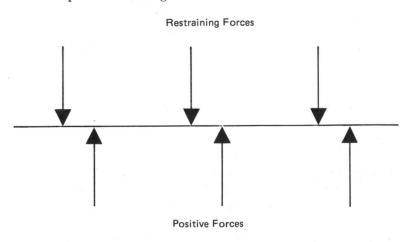

Figure 4.1 *Force-field analysis*

One problem which arises in evaluating various solutions is *disagreements*. Sometimes these arise because there are no facts to support either side or the team is unsure about various points in the solution. More information and better analysis may help. Alternatively, there may be conflicts of values. Then the team can split into groups and implement different solutions simultaneously, or find a compromise which allows agreed action but avoids disputed actions. Crosby (1972, p. 18) suggests that the important point is to approach disagreements in an 'enquiry mode', which involves (rather than trying to convince others that one member is right) trying to find out about the differing views. He argues that enquirers should ask the following questions:

1. Do I understand your viewpoint correctly?
2. What assumptions or opinions or facts do you have that cause you to take that point of view?
3. What information can we request from available resources to help our enquiry?

I have previously given an example of using the enquiry mode (p. 44) and the idea will reappear in later chapters.

Having analysed problems and solutions and decided on an appropriate course of action, the team can *implement* it, remembering the importance of feedback if more than one person is involved. Often a particular job can be given to one member of the team, in which case action is relatively straightforward. If, however, work is to be shared, the team faces issues of task differentiation and role integration; these provide two other ways of team-building.

Team-building through task differentiation

Some teams would like to clarify or change the way in which tasks are defined and divided between team members. Where they are happy with their roles, this can clear up border disputes; where roles are unclear, this can be the first stage in role integration and setting up priority or specialisation systems.

Agencies can divide up tasks in a variety of ways; they often choose one and then have to live with its conflicts with the other possibilities. For example, a community project organised its workers into domains of living (see pp. 54–5). One ran a housing and welfare-rights centre, another did youth work, a third worked with community groups and the last with trade unions. Equally possible splits were into client characteristics (West Indian, Asian, Irish, indigenous white), client groups (individuals, families, formed groups, community groups), or problem categories (unemployment, housing, income maintenance). Each of these overlaps in different ways. During the project the youth worker found himself working with unemployed West Indian youths in a club. This limited the use he could make of welfare-rights advice, the possibility of working with family problems, and involvement through trade unions in employment issues. Task differentiation in this (and every other) case limited the options; working out tasks can bring to light many opportunities in a team.

Defining tasks and skills

Table 4.1 compares a number of different systems for differentiating tasks. Although they are broadly similar, there are differences in emphasis. For example, BASW has a professional association's interest in carving out a large territory and covers the widest range. Jeans was producing a research instrument for research into SSD teams, and tends to differentiate assessment tasks which are important in these agencies, and his 'modifying' is a pale shadow of BASW or Teare and McPheeters, who expect social workers to be directly involved in social action. Tasks are defined in terms of work with or for clients: manager, administrator and consultant means managing workloads and resources and consulting with clients rather than managing an agency or staff. I have not included the lengthy definitions (for which refer to the original texts), but the groupings of comparisons should somewhere cover terms which explain the more obscure items. Each of these systems provides a comprehensive list of tasks to remind teams of the possible range when they are working on tasks: they can use a complete system, or devise their own, using existing systems to check that they have covered everything.

Table 4.1 *Different analyses of social work tasks*

Teare and McPheeters (1970)	BASW (1977)	Baker (1976a)	Jeans (1978)
	I. Tasks about which writers agree		
Advocate	Advocate	Advocate	Advocacy
Teacher/trainer	Social/public educator	Educator	Teaching
Behaviour changer	@Attitude/behaviour changer	Therapist	Behaviour changing
Consultant	@Consultant	Consultant	Offering consultation
Care-giver	Care-giver	Caretaker	Care-giver
	II. Tasks about which most writers agree		
Broker	Mediator	Broker	Linking
		Mediator	
Mobiliser	Mobiliser of resources		Mobilising
Administrator	@Director/manager	Administrator	Other
Community planner	Agent of social change/regulation		Modifying
	III. Tasks where there is some agreement		
	Adviser	Adviser	
	Researcher	Researcher	
	Enabler	Enabler	
	Protector		Protecting clients
		Co-ordinator	Co-ordinating
	IV. Tasks which different writers differentiate more or less fully		
Evaluator	@Diagnostician		Reviewing
	@Planner		Investigating
			Evaluating
	V. Additional tasks		
Outreach			
	Clarifier		
	@Counsellor		
		Supporter	

Note: BASW designates tasks marked thus: @ as those which should be performed by a qualified social worker.

Another useful aspect of task analysis is looking at skills. Teare and McPheeters (1970) suggest that three factors affect how skilful workers need to be for particular jobs: *complexity* — the number of variables involved; *difficulty* — the number of different skills and amount of knowledge involved; and *risk* — how vulnerable the client is if the worker fails. Some jobs contain equal proportions of these. Some tend towards one or the other. For example, checking on whether a baby has been battered is not complex or difficult but it is very risky, and therefore needs a lot of skill. On the other hand, representing clients at social security tribunals is not risky, but it is complex and difficult. Stamp, quoted by Jeans (1978), is concerned with two factors: how much judgement the situation requires (and consequently how much autonomy the worker needs), and how much the worker needs and is able to follow predetermined procedures or act creatively. The less easy it is to prescribe what to do in a situation in advance, the more necessary it is to have a high level of skill and creativity.

Using task and skill analysis

Task and skill analysis can be used in individual cases to decide among a group of workers sharing the case who should do what, and can be codified into an allocation system (see pp. 57–9). For team-building purposes, however, I am concerned with ways in which the team can jointly analyse tasks and skills.

One way is to use an instrument like that of Jeans (1978) to survey the work of each team member and create personal profiles of the tasks they normally undertake. Jeans found considerable differences between apparently similar workers. Less detailed, but quicker, team members can rate themselves or each other on their normal style of work and what they would prefer to do. Different categories of work can also be rated to see what tasks are involved. The systems can be adapted to community, residential and group work if these are the team's foci of attention.

 Looking at these in a team, some relevant questions might be: Are there tasks nobody does? Who specialises in which tasks? Do particular tasks go together? Are particular tasks or groups of tasks particularly useful for particular client groups, client problems or community needs? Does the team's task profile relate to the needs of clients and cases revealed in the analysis? Do team members' actual task profiles match their preferred profiles? Answers to this question might involve training, to enable team members to take up new or enhanced tasks, or may lead to changes in priorities, specialisation and work allocation, which I shall examine next.

Team-building through role integration

Role integration is the process of clustering tasks together into roles which make sense and allocating those roles to individuals in ways which create sensible domains for them. This involves, first, deciding *priorities*, because the team or agency will need to decide which are the most important factors in the work; *specialisation*, because roles will determine an individual's domain and this rapidly becomes a specialism in one sense or another (see pp. 90—3); and *workload allocation* follows logically because if the team's workload changes at all it will have to be sorted out into specialisms, given a priority and allocated to a worker's domain. ⟍

Devising a system

There are a variety of systems for dealing with these processes, mostly related to SSDs. A comprehensive review with case examples is contained in Parsloe (1981). Day *et al.* (1978), describing the implementation of Hall's (1975b) OPS system in a team, shows how such schemes can clarify and encourage teamwork, and that is why I am proposing their use as a way of team-building. However, teams may find them rather complex or unsuited to their needs. They often require a good grasp of very complex structures and terminology, and many people find them difficult to follow (e.g. some of Day *et al.*'s team). Often, value judgements concerning, say, vulnerability or feasibility are cast into rather dubious numerical weightings or categories. These should be the result of shared judgements, but I have sometimes seen such schemes operated on the judgements of one or two dominant team members.

It may be better, therefore, for team members to devise their own schemes, perhaps with reference to existing systems or by working through a comprehensive categorisation of social work activities which is independent of such systems. One of these which I find useful is given by Teare and McPheeters (1970), and I have set out their ideas in abbreviated form in Table 4.2.

There are three sets of factors: domains of living; how well people, groups or communities are working; and the obstacles that get in the way of satisfactory life. Social work activities are directed at some combination of aspects of this framework, one from each list, and they vary depending on the

Table 4.2   *Frameworks of social welfare activities*

Domains of living	States of functioning	Obstacles to functioning

Physical functioning
Emotional functioning
Learning, training, development
Occupational functioning
Financial
Mobility
Group functioning (e.g. in the family)
Shelter (housing)
Safety/protection (physical, political)
Spiritual functioning
Aesthetic functioning
Leisure/recreation
	Continuum covering
	  well-being
	  stress
	  problems
	  crisis
	  disability
		Catastrophes
		Rigid laws, regulations
		Environmental
		  deficiencies
		Personal deficiencies

Source: adapted from Teare and McPheeters (1970).

combination. For example, working with people who are in a crisis (e.g. unemployment) in their world of work (i.e. occupational functioning), because of environmental deficiencies (e.g. mass unemployment due to recession), is different from working with people who are suffering stress because of financial difficulties due to their personal deficiencies. Vary any one of the three factors in each of these two examples and a different mode of action is implied.

Teare and McPheeters outline five ways in which work activities might be clustered. These are the target (e.g. the clients' problems, domain of living), the objectives of the work, the worker (e.g. skills or interests), the tasks and skills already discussed, and the work setting (e.g. residential, day care or types of supervision).

Priorities

Using this framework a team can decide where its work is concentrated and where each individual concentrates; each of the three factors and their interaction can be examined. Similarly, it is possible to look at the clientele and decide how these people fall into the three groups, and I have already said that task profiles can also be examined against the team's work to see in which ways they match. From this, various priorities can be worked out. Which domains of living are more important? At what points on the status-of-functioning continuum does the agency concentrate? A community work agency might concentrate on well-being; a preventive one on stress and problems; a casework agency on crisis and disability. And the same applies to obstacles to functioning. Setting up priority systems in this way is the basis of many existing team-building efforts (e.g. Bush, 1980).

Specialisation

With a set of priorities a team can look at the work patterns of its members. The aim will be to cluster various tasks into roles so that the priorities of the team are met. Teare and McPheeters argue that specialisation should be organised around the client's rather than the worker's needs, but this is not an argument for a client-group system of specialisation. There is already a great deal of specialisation by setting (e.g. residential, day care, fieldwork, probation, hospital, community project), by mode of social work (e.g. group work, community work, casework), by worker interest or skill (e.g. family therapy, group work), or by geographical division (e.g. patch systems, petty sessional divisions), which may limit opportunities for very detailed client-groups specialisation. For example, in a probation area there may be enough cases to permit one worker to build up experience in dealing with sexual offenders, but the division into patch-based teams, prison welfare, hostel liaison or community service may prevent these being brought together so that one worker can deal with them all.

In finding specialisations the team needs to identify a framework for dividing up its work (often domains of living in fieldwork, obstacles to functioning in community work) and can then work out criteria (e.g. training, interest) for allocating them to workers. Large clusters of activity can be divided among several workers, or one worker can take on several small clusters.

There are problems with this. Priority-setting tends to produce status differences, so that if work has a low priority workers who take it on tend to be seen as being of low status (or may only be employed on a low status or salary). Workers who have some low- and some high-status work may move towards the latter. Moreover, taking on one specialisation can limit (or perhaps expand) workers' future opportunities and there may well be staffing problems. The second problem is that boundaries between the clusters might not be very clear so that there are problems of overlap. Systems of priority and specialisation are therefore usually tied up with a work-allocation system which deals with boundary problems. The individual problems of maintaining specialist roles are considered further in Chapter 6.

Allocation of workload

Allocation systems use the same bases as priority and special-isation systems to define cases and allocate them to workers. *Patch systems* (Hadley and McGath, 1979) give all the cases in a small locality to one worker or a small group. This emphasises community responsiveness, but it may mean that specialised client needs are harder to meet, and variations in workload between workers on different patches can be hard to control.

All other allocation systems involve at least three elements, and a system can be intended to vary the proportional import-ance of these elements according to the needs of the team. First, allocation systems may be concerned to promote *equality of involvement* in the process of allocation by mem-bers of the team; sometimes, however, this matters relatively little to them. Second, systems may be concerned with making the decision more or less *public*. Third, there will be a concern with *certainty*; sometimes it is useful to have a clear record of who has been given what, while in other teams a certain vagueness has its advantages. Some people assume all these three things go together, but this is not necessarily so. For example, one team in an SSD decided to change from a system where the senior allocated cases to one where a team meeting made a joint decision. They thought that equality of involvement, public awareness in the team of decisions and therefore greater certainty about what was going on would follow. Alas, most of them found the system rather confusing, and the allocation records broke down, so certainty was lost; some thought that decision-making was less fair because it was dominated by a few voices, rather than the relatively neutral team leader. So in this case certainty and equality did not ensue from the more public scheme; each of these characteristics had to be separately worked for.

Planning allocation systems involves considering what the team needs and wants to take into account when it makes allocation decisions. Any one of the specific allocation systems reviewed by Parsloe (1981) offers useful detailed suggestions, but again teams may like to devise a system which suits their own needs rather than follow an unsuitable pattern. Among the factors that will need to be considered in such a case are the levels of skill involved in the work to be done (which can be measured according to the amount of discretion which the worker will need in order to do the work), the kind and amount of supervision that the worker will need and where it will come from, the client's needs and characteristics (e.g. who will he best respond to?), the standards and expectations of the agency and related agencies, and the team's priorities and specialisation system.

The team will also need to consider the objectives of their system: Is it to implement a set of priorities, or encourage particular forms of specialisation, or provide a mechanism for delegation? How should it balance equality, publicity and certainty? In a four-person community work team, for example, requests for help and involvement, and developments in existing activities, were discussed in a weekly review of activities and then rather vaguely shared out. A lot of mutual involvement in the work was needed. This system stressed equality and publicity of involvement, but certainty was less important. The main aims were delegation (or sharing) and keeping to a set of priorities. In a probation team, to take another rather different example, the system was reviewed and a set of allocation criteria agreed, but allocations were in fact made by the senior. In this case, because nearly all work came as a result of demands from outside the team which *had* to be met in some way, a priorities system was necessary, and specialisation was fairly well defined and relatively unchanging. Delegation was the most important aim. Certainty (and speed) in allocation was the main essential; the team were satisfied with equality in setting up the system, and did not want it in its day-to-day running; and since the work was fairly individualised, publicity of allocation did not matter, since any conflicts or overlaps could be picked up by a fairly uncomplicated administrative system.

In general, fairly non-specialised settings where work must be shared, like community work and residential care, often need a system concentrating on priorities, equality and publicity, while specialised and individualised settings, such as many day-care establishments (where work is done in specialised groups) and casework agencies, need systems which provide clarity in delegation and specialisation with certainty, and only enough publicity to deal with weaknesses in their administrative systems.

All this is, of course, time-consuming. A team could have a conference of two or three days, or a series of half-days in which a series of possible systems can be tried out in simulation by the team on some existing cases to see if the right results appear.

So far I have considered methods of allocation involving the whole team which deal with problems of specialisation and priorities. An alternative is to concentrate on a more personal basis by sharing work, either on the margins of specialisms, across particular specialist or work divisions, or simply between workers whose tasks seem to fit together. Sharing leads to the subject of the next chapter which is concerned with how individuals manage their relationships with one another in work groups and teams.

Team meetings

A team meeting is a central aspect of teamwork; many team-building methods that I have discussed rely on meetings as a vehicle. And yet team meetings are often troubled affairs.

Many people dislike meetings if they are not firmly chaired and led so that they keep to the point; if there is not clear purpose or focus; if people do not do what they agreed to do; if one person or group dominates discussions or have hidden purposes or personal aims in conflict with the overt aim of the meeting; and if people come unprepared to the meeting (Dyer, 1977, pp. 74—5).

Teams can find it useful to review their meetings from time to time to see if such problems exist. Dealing with them may partly mean that individuals will have to behave efficiently, and behaviour in the meeting will have to be controlled by effective chairmanship. Changes in the structure of meetings may be appropriate. A series of team meetings or part-team meetings with focused subject-matter may be better than one general team meeting. One community work agency, for example, has four meetings: a decision-making and review group which allows those working on various projects to share and plan their activities; a meeting of all staff concerned with discussions about their position as employees, the agency's position in the community, and shared issues; an administrative and clerical staff meeting; and a meeting dealing with the management and financing of the agency. As well as firm chairing of such meetings (not necessarily by the most senior person present — rotation encourages equality of contribution and helps people feel it is a *staff* meeting), one useful strategy is to record in the notes who is to take what action by what date, and to check what has happened at the next meeting.

Team or individual development

Because this chapter is concerned with team development as a group, the individual contribution has been rather artificially ignored. Many teams do approach problems as a group and encourage individual development in that context. Several times, however, individual consequences, attitudes and relationships have been relevant. Some teams progress through concentrating on individual development and work-sharing. This may be particularly relevant to the kinds of teams where more collaborative structures are not wanted or not appropriate.

Teams can develop, therefore, through individuals making changes and affecting others through the way they share their own work, rather than by general team-building, and this approach may be easier for people whose colleagues do not share their enthusiasm for teamwork, or where the tasks of a team do not make more collaborative activities relevant. It is to the alternative, individual, approach that I turn in the next chapter.

5

The Individual and the Team

This chapter looks at individuals' relationships with others in a team. In Chapter 4 I suggested that encouraging sharing was a way of moving to a more collaborative style of teamwork in the group, as such sharing increased, and this is examined towards the end of this chapter. The first section discusses what individuals bring to a work group. The second section considers how relationships might be established and developed. The third looks at ways of dealing with relationship problems which often arise in teams. Finally, these sections are a foundation for the subsequent discussion of promoting sharing.

What the individual brings to the team

⟨Brill (1976) suggests that members of a team have four functions: the *tasks* that they undertake, their specialist *role*, their *position* in the interpersonal relationships of the team, and their *person*, which refers to their personal characteristics and history. It is these two last aspects of their contribution to the team that are emphasised here, as the first two were in the last chapter, but their importance lies partly in the contribution they make to how roles and tasks are integrated and differentiated. /Because position and person affect how team members behave, understanding their own position and person, and those of others in the team, is useful for team members. It can never be complete, and we are always learning about ourselves and everyone else around us, but thinking about this carefully may help team members to avoid some problems which otherwise might arise.

The person

Brill suggests seven personal characteristics which team members might find it useful to think about. They are given, in ascending order of privacy, in Table 5.1, though all of them are of course more or less visible to others. All these characteristics affect one another, and may be more or less important in particular circumstances. For example, my generalist skill in playing the piano was worthless in my social work career until I happened to get involved with an old people's home needing an accompanist for singing evenings. The existence of some characteristics often blinds people to others. For instance, I once worked with a social worker whose experience was mainly with the elderly and handicapped. He also had experience in another place at another time as a foster parent, but neither he nor others had recognised that this might be valuable in child-care work until a foster-parent group was proposed and he mentioned his interest in attending. Often, latent characteristics and behaviour patterns are ignored in this way. The way someone feels about their age or sex, or about conventions of dress and politeness are relevant to how others see them and how they behave towards others.

The position

In any group people take up, or are pushed into, positions. Brill gives six examples, all of which in my experience are quite common: the leader, the fighter, the catalyst, the know-it-all, the manipulator, the peacemaker. There is often a joker, a radical, an activist and a representative of the silent majority. Sometimes people occupy positions because of their personality or characteristics and will tend to be the same in many groups they are members of. Often, on the other hand, roles are taken up and reinforced by how individuals are seen by others. As team membership or circumstances change, differ-

Table 5.1 *Personal factors in team membership*

	Factor	Comment	Example
Least private	Specialist knowledge and skill	Related to work	Social work training, experience as foster parent
	Generalist knowledge and skill	Not related to work	Piano-playing, woodwork
	Reference groups	Groups aspired to or valued	Professional groups, political party
	Latent characteristics	Natural characteristics of team member	Age, sex, race, religion, class
	Behaviour patterns and norms	Typical behaviour and socialised expectations	Dress, courtesy, loyalty, use of authority
	Values and attitudes	Attitudes to how human beings are and should be	Worth of human life, 'everyone can grow'
Most private	Self-image	How team members see themselves	Helpers, do-gooders, competent, worthless

ent roles are picked up. Much of the effect of this comes from stereotyping which is strengthened sometimes by the interaction of roles. For example, I tend to act in many groups as a stimulator-fighter-catalyst, presenting ideas in a fairly aggressive way to jolt others. If *my* other roles or if other roles *in the group* affect it, I tone down this typical behaviour. When I am teaching, for example, or representing a range of views, I tend to be more evenhanded and neutral in style, as is the case when I find others retreat, or if there is no one there to act as opposition or as peacemaker. Similarly my behaviour often stimulates another person to be peacemaker when this is not their usual style. In groups where there is another aggressive person, I have often been stimulated to act as peacemaker.

Thinking about person and position

Systematic self-disclosure by a joint discussion of each other as a planned way of team-building may be unhelpful, because the effects are rather indirect and some people in the team will be more prepared for it than others.[A useful approach for people interested in developing teamwork is to be aware of these factors, to take them into account when dealing with others, to think about them in relation to themselves and to be open about their own attitudes and responses to others *only when it is directly relevant to a piece of work.*] I have slowly been learning to do this, and I think most people find it helpful and respond well to it. I have also discovered that most other people are well aware of things I thought I had fairly well-contained. The right limit seems to be when I feel uncomfortable about raising something. That is the point at which to stop. This only applies to personal self-disclosure, not to information about the work or feedback to subordinates on their performance, which of course may have to be discussed, however uncomfortable this is.

Occasionally, a more structured way of increasing self-disclosure in a team can be useful when team members think that they do not understand the attitudes, experience or priorities of others, or in a new group which is all-agreeable to some kind of self-disclosing exercise. Such an exercise should allow people to limit what they wish to disclose. A person's preference not to reveal should not even be questioned. Sometimes discussions can be organised with another team member and the pair can support each other in deciding what it is appropriate to disclose. A number of self-disclosure exercises exist (see Brandes and Phillips, 1979; Merry and Allerhand, 1977; Woodcock, 1979) but perhaps the most useful is the Johari window. It is fully discussed by Merry and Allerhand (1977) and is particularly useful here because it is concerned with showing differences in perception of others or of a problem in a group. The window is shown in Figure 5.1.

For sharing information in a team, each member privately lists their own and everyone else's strengths and liabilities (or any other categories of information). These are (anony-

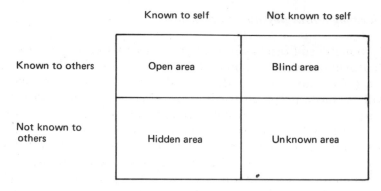

Figure 5.1   *The Johari window*

mously) given to a leader, who makes a Johari window for each person from the information provided by others to compare with the one they make for themselves. This exercise also helps people sort out doubts about themselves; it can be very encouraging. For the problem-solving exercise everyone makes a list of what only they know about the problem, and then what is known to themselves and others. These are tabulated by the leader; each individual works out from this what is in their blind area and how this changes their perception of the problem. An outsider can sometimes draw attention to issues in the unknown area.

Establishing and managing relationships

Any team member must establish their person and position and manage their relationships within the group. There are three aspects to this: understanding and becoming part of the team structures, boundary-setting, and terminating and changing relationships.

Structures and relationships

The six aspects of team structure (p. 20) can be used to understand where and how to fit into a team. Who *communicates* most with a member and how? Who has *powers* and in what way? Who *likes* whom and what are the effects? How do team members' *roles* affect each other? How does *work flow* between members? What are people's *status* in relation to others, and on what basis is it? Understanding structures can help members to decide what structure they should use in building relationships/ For example, I like talking to colleagues a great deal (communicating). Some people think this is gossiping, so when I detect irritation I use the work-flow approach, finding work which I can pass on to, take from or share with colleagues to build contacts.

Some structures can be used to overcome others. If someone is disliked, for example, work flow, emphasising roles and communication can reduce the limitations that this places on teamwork, though it may not change the liking pattern.

Boundaries and relationships

There are four kinds of boundary relationships between team members, and these can produce a variety of problems.

Mutual relationships occur when the boundaries between two people's roles are consistent. Usually, they are mutually agreed, and trying to create mutual boundaries is an important objective of many team-building exercises. If this cannot be done jointly, it can finally be achieved by members negotiating separately with each other over geographical areas, client groups, methods of work, and any other aspects discussed in Chapter 4. If this does not work out, members can set out and try to defend their own boundaries through a personal task and skill analysis. A simple personal example: as a social worker in an SSD I dealt with many families with adolescents, but felt I was not skilful at dealing with pre-school children. A colleague was, so we came to an arrangement whereby if an adolescent in one of my families had a baby, I would treat this as a separate family and we would either work jointly or divide the case.

Overlapping boundaries where team members' roles cover the same territory are very common. For example, the work-load in some specialities may be too great for one person, or two people need to gain experience of the work (which helps continuity in the team). The main problem is invasion, which may help to break down unnecessary boundaries, but can lead to hostility and jealousy. Again, task and skill analysis can help to divide a domain sensibly, and if invasion occurs, recognition helps (e.g. advance discussion, or apology afterwards).

Parallel boundaries sometimes occur in which people work in the same domain but do not share any work at all. One SSD team, for example, had two workers specialising with the elderly in different staff groups, working in different ways. Although they could have supported each other, complemented each other's skills and jointly promoted the needs of the elderly, they worked entirely separately. Promoting joint discussion of shared issues and interests and ways around such differences may help to create overlapping or mutal boundaries. Alternatively, joint interests can be created (e.g. in this case for each to represent the other in negotiating with housing allocations or admissions to old people's homes in liaison arrangements).

Finally, *distant* boundaries often exist where there are gaps between team members' roles. One way around this is to find work which falls in the gap but nearer to the interests of one or the other and allocate it accordingly, so that the gap is slowly removed. Joint working on cases where different client groups are involved in the same family, or people in different areas are connected in some way, might also help.

In all these problems sometimes a complete reorganisation of task and skill boundaries can help. For example, in one probation team, work was reorganised from a geographical basis to a legislative division into probation work, after-care and matrimonial work. In one SSD team, work for social work assistants was reorganised from a client-group basis (elderly, handicapped, families) to a task and skill basis (assessment, emotional support, teaching and advice-giving).

Changing and terminating relationships

Since, inevitably, relationships change and team members come and go, a system for regular review can avoid boundary and structural problems. As team members leave, it is useful for them to review either jointly, with a colleague, or with the team leader, depending on the style of the team, their boundaries with each team member, and their place in each team structure. Sometimes it is possible to do this alone and then make arrangements individually with others to correct any problems.

Problems with team relationships

This section considers some relationships in teams which are often seen as difficult to handle or problematic. I have one general rule on dealing with relationship problems: talk about them. This is not easy because the people involved in relationships do not always know when it is best to discuss them, or it is too painful, and outsiders may have no way of raising questions. A helpful way of initiating discussion without inappropriate conflict is to use the enquiry mode (see p. 50). This involves seeking information about the views, assumptions and opinions of others, and behaving in a way that assumes everyone wants to seek a way out of the difficulty. Similarly, disclosing information about reactions rather than judgements can help avoid hostile exchanges.

The remaining part of this section discusses these general points in relation to problems grouped around different ways of looking at team structure.

Problems with communications

Assessing communication problems. Many difficulties in teams are put down to communication problems — either people do not know what someone should have told them, or there is too much to be communicated. The problems can arise in different parts of the communication system, however, so in assessing problems teams need to look at the communication system.

First, there is the *message*. Is the amount of material too much to understand, or too little to meet the need, or is it difficult material to communicate? What information needs to be communicated? Is it available? If not, how can it be obtained?)

Second, we have the *communicators*. Are senders of messages in the right positions in the team, acceptable to receivers, and with the right skills and personality to put the message across? Are receivers able to get the point of communication, or are there distractions, lack of motivation, poor understanding, which get in the way? Does hierarchical position make a difference?

Third, there is the *method* of communication. Is it, or should it be, in writing or verbal, to a particular person or group or to all concerned? If it is verbal, the structure will include the verbal system (words and sentence structure), intonation (inflexions, emphases, breaks in speech), para-linguistics (e.g. ums, ahs, coughs, laughter) and kinesics (eye contact, body language) (Fraser, 1978a). All of these will affect how communications work.

\Communications are ways of controlling relationships, conveying personal and social identity, status and power, and all these can affect how information is conveyed, because any communication will contain a variety of possible meanings and barriers to communication\

Promoting communication. Having assessed the problems, a team or members concerned about communication can concentrate on specific parts of communication, rather than scattering their efforts. One way is for members individually and collectively to promote what Ends and Page (1977) suggest are the right attitudes for good communication: fairness and integrity rather than manipulativeness, openness, constructive and optimistic attitudes rather than carping, striving for equality in the social relationships around communication and being receptive to and respecting the views of others.

Communication activities in a team can be particularly helpful in those teams where collaborative team-building is not needed. If the problem is the *message* — either too much information or too little — projects for organising and sharing responsibility for keeping and supplying information, research for information about the area, clients, aspects of practice or policy issues, can all be helpful. Presenting results through visual aids, role plays or documents should be lively and involve all team members.

Where *methods* or *personalities* are a problem, communication exercises are possible. Some examples (from Merry and Allerhand, 1977) are as follows. The team is grouped in threes: a speaker, an observer and a listener. The speaker makes a point about a team problem and the listener has to summarise it to the satisfaction of the speaker and observer, and when he has satisfied both that he has accurately understood it he can say what he thinks about the statement. From time to time they change roles. This gets opinions about a problem stated in a logical way, and arguments and judgements about people's views can also be made explicit. More important, at the end of the exercise the team can discuss what made it hard to listen, what kept attention, what distracted listeners, what people learned about themselves as speakers and listeners. These can be listed as general points, and taken up by specific individuals privately.

Another exercise involves trying different ways of communicating. The team agrees that items at its meetings, or at a special conference, must be presented in one of five different ways:

(a) as a written report
(b) as an oral report
(c) as a dialogue between two team members
(d) demonstrated by an active presentation
(e) drawn as a diagram, flow-chart or file of visual material

The first item in the meeting has to be by (a), the second (b), and so on. Each presentation can be clarified and questioned. This encourages practice in different styles of communication, and enables them to be compared. It is also fun.

Problems with power structure

Assessing power problems. In Chapter 2 I examined the variety of different structures by which power can be divided in a team, deriving from the different bases from which power is drawn. Inevitably the variety of possibilities lead to problems if some people in the team feel that the wrong pattern, or the wrong source of power, is being used.

Problems often arise in three areas. First, *dominance* and *submission* must be considered. Some people think power is mainly concerned with who wins in the event of a dispute. If some people always win, their dominance and the submission of others may become a problem, particularly if the dominant person is not the leader or one sanctioned by the leader, or if one person always tends to win. The general trend of dominance may be more important than individual arguments. A minor matter may be the last straw for a team which has not been upset by earlier issues which objectively are more imperfect. On the other hand, a triumph by a person over a minor matter does not necessarily mean that he or she will generally dominate the overall relationship. So, if there appears to be unreasonable anxiety about a minor decision, dominance trends may be a problem. Teams might also look at whether a person's or group's dominance derives from personality (their push for their position, or the preference of others for submission), from the use of resources (rewards, sanctions, the ability to withdraw without disadvantage), or are reinforced by the structure and hierarchy of the agency. Dominance and submission can be seen, then, as part of the pattern of team relationships.

A second difficult area is *power and responsibility*, which tend to go together because a person usually acquires powers either because they are needed to fulfil responsibilities, or because they are prepared to accept responsibility. Having responsibility without power often means that jobs are not properly carried out; having power but not accepting the concomitant responsibilities often leads to resentment. A way of checking these is to list as many responsibilities of individuals as possible and consider whether in practice (as opposed to theory) they have the resources and rights to carry them out; if not, there is a misalignment.

The third problem is that power is related to *social structures*, and tends to persist in existing patterns, along class and status lines, so people can be frustrated because things are difficult to change, or people may have the trappings of power and responsibility without sanctions or duties to back them.

A useful way of assessing these issues is to review power in the team. Team members could look at a recently made important decision and ask how all these issues were dealt with; alternatively, they could list a set of issues and try to produce three examples of recent team behaviour in each case to support their assessment of how the team works. Table 5.2 offers a format for looking at these issues through a series of questions.

Table 5.2 *Questions about the use of power in a team*

---

1. Who is always or often dominant in team discussion?
2. Who is always or often submissive in team discussion?
3. Is the pattern of dominance or submission due to (a) personality or socialisation, (b) resources, rewards, or sanctions, or (c) hierarchical powers and responsibilities?
4. Do people have responsibilities but not the right personality, resources or power to carry them out?
5. Do people have capacities which they do not have the power or responsibility to use?
6. Do people use the right to instruct or direct activities when other people think this is inappropriate?
7. Are important disagreements resolved by the use of power rather than by mutual agreement?

Dealing with power problems. Four strategies offer some possibilities for changing power problems.

Changing personal style can help if personality is the problem. An individual can decide to change his own pattern of submission or dominance, and this will affect how others behave; if my behaviour is not submissive, you cannot be so dominating. Colleagues can agree to support each other by feeding back their view of the behaviour of others.

Resources can sometimes be changed. Managers can remove or add sanctions or rewards or change their allocation. Team members can devalue some rewards (e.g. if power is misused to achieve a quiet life, by producing unquiet reactions to misuse and supporting helpful use).

Alternative structures, such as unions or professional associations, or meetings with senior management, can sometimes be used to bring sanctions into play to change existing patterns of power. The responsibility and power assessments described above can help to provide good arguments for these.

Finally, *relationships* can be used to emphasise a powerful person's responsibility for a subordinate's personal development and combat the misuse of power, or to use shared activities, working in an enquiry mode to alter existing power relationships. Similarly a worker who is loath to accept responsibility can be helped by involvement and encouragement.

Problems with liking and conflict

Teamwork promotes close relationships and so liking or conflict can easily arise, with helpful and unhelpful consequences.

Liking, love and sexual attraction. Liking relationships in a team are helpful because people who like one another will be more motivated to deal with problems and work together. There are problems, too, because people who like one another can seem to *exclude* others in the team or outsiders whom they like less, and easily to *influence* each other, so others may feel mistreated in power relationships.

Liking can grow into love and sexual attraction. Although many people in a team regard this a private matter, it rebounds on others because exclusivity and influence can be even stronger, and there is sometimes an element of 'immorality' (e.g. extra-marital relationships) which can provoke strong feelings — as can particular forms of attraction or sexual behaviour (e.g. homosexuality or using pornography).

Liking and attraction imply disliking and repulsion. If people dislike or are sexually repelled by others, this may cause hidden conflicts.

Some people argue that all this should be kept out of working life, but this is impossible because liking, disliking, attraction and repulsion affect how everyone reacts to one another. There may be sexual and associated status overtones to all kinds of relationships. For example, most supervisors in social work are men, most subordinates women. This reinforces and is reinforced by the traditional male—female, dominance—submission pattern, and may provoke sexual feelings (positive or negative) or rejection of the position, depending on the participants' views. When there is a female supervisor, some difficulties may arise because it is not the conventional arrangement.

Dealing with these problems is not easy. A *general review* of the issues and people's views about them may be helpful in a collaborative team if there is no problem at present. If there is no problem, I suggest that people enjoy their likes and dislikes inexplicitly. When people feel that a relationship is causing difficulty, discussing it among the whole team is unhelpful, because most people find it an invasion of their own or others' privacy. It is better to *raise concerns* with one of the parties to a relationship separately (if they are together, a hostile confrontation sometimes results because they feel they must support each other), and invite them to raise it with the other. Implying that other members of the team have discussed it and have sent a representative may provoke anxiety. If they have discussed it, it might be better for each member to raise their anxieties separately with the parties of their choice.

Finally, people who are involved in problematic liking or disliking relationships can organise themselves to *limit exclusivity and influence*, by openly acknowledging to others that they realise the problems exist, and explicitly avoiding the problems or discussing them when they come up. It helps other people to feel they can raise difficulties if the parties concerned take a lead. These issues should particularly be dealt with where a husband and wife work together, since people often feel inhibited in affecting the relationship in any way, or where formal hierarchical relationships may inhibit people (e.g. a supervisor—subordinate relationship).

Conflict. As with liking, conflict is not always a problem. Some conflict between people in teams can have benefits for an agency. Walton (1969), on whose work this section is based, says benefits arise from conflict where it creates efforts at solving problems or innovation; helps people's understanding of criticism and refinement of their views; strengthens their self-confidence; and helps to work out their internal conflicts. Conflict may sometimes become troublesome, where it reduces the will to do important things, creates unchangeable patterns of interaction in the team, or apparently distorts perceptions of and reactions to the needs of clients or the team.

Walton suggests that conflict is cyclical. A number of *issues* exist in any relationship which might cause conflict, but there are few problems until a *triggering event* brings the issues into play. Conflict *behaviour* appears as the team tries to deal with the trigger and this affects how the issues and triggering event are settled. Conflict behaviour may mean that either the issues are not properly resolved and are likely to recur, or other issues are more easily triggered into conflict. As there are more experiences of conflict, more issues arise which are likely to cause it, and triggering events lead to conflict when, previously, they would have been relatively neutral in effect.

Substantive issues (about real problems) which often arise include philosophical differences, role invasion, task deprivation, where people are unable to do their work because others do not assist them. *Emotional issues* (arising from feelings about others) which often arise include deprivation of personal satisfaction in various ways, incompatible personal style which irritate other team members. Dyer (1977) suggests that conflicts often derive from unfulfilled expectations in a team, and assumptions and expectations should be looked at in a conflict to see if they are reasonable.

Even where issues exist, normal social conventions prevent conflict arising. Getting involved in conflict may waste time when people want to get on with their work; most people may expect that there will be no arguments; people may have an idea about themselves that they do not get into conflicts either generally or with particular people such as subordinates; people may feel the need to maintain a public image of equanimity (many managers feel that this is important — so do some social workers in dealing with clients); one member may think that another is too vulnerable or risky to attack; or the way the team is organised reduces interaction, so conflict is held in check. Triggering events take away these normal social *barriers to conflict.*

Conflict in organisations and teams usually results in ambivalent behaviour. Feelings of conflict (anger, attack, rejection) and competitive strategies (blocking, interruptions, alliances, manoeuvring) are balanced by feelings of regret, sympathy, perhaps guilt and co-operative strategies aimed at ending the conflict. Few people sustain all-out war.

Filley (1975, pp. 9–12) suggests nine kinds of social relationships which often lead to conflict: ambiguous domains where there is uncertainty over who is responsible for what; conflicts of interest; communication barriers caused by separation in time or space; one party depends on another; where there is a lot of differentiation of roles in the organisation; where the parties have many dealings with one another; where there is need for consensus; where there are regulations about particular forms of behaviour; and where there is a history of past conflict. One way of *preventing conflict* is to reduce the relationships in which these problems can cause difficulty. Teams could look for these to see if they are causing problems which lead to conflict. They could also try to strengthen barriers to conflict and reduce triggering events.

Once a conflict starts, the situation can become confused because issues get dragged into the argument. This happens in a number of ways. *Umbrella* issues are used because they seem more legitimate than the real issue, e.g. substantive issues are brought in to cover emotional ones. *Facsimiles* are issues which are similar to but safer than the main point. Looking at the apparent issue in a dispute which seems unreasonably emotional can give clues to other similar issues which may be so strongly felt that the parties to the dispute cannot even talk about them. *Bundling boards* are issues which are added by the parties to fuel the flames; they use them to emphasise how different from each other they are. *Seizing the high ground* can sometimes set off a covert conflict because one party, seeing an issue which will probably lead to a dispute, acts before conflict starts to seize an advantage. The fact of this advantage may then become an issue which covers the main debate. Sometimes, *self-defence* acts in the same way. People feel threatened and so act defensively. This makes others feel guilty or that something is being hidden and the issue seems to become the defensive-ness.

In general, then, substantive conflicts easily lead to emotion-al conflicts, and emotional conflicts tend to lead people to find issues that will divide them. It is not necessarily true to say that dealing with conflict only needs resolution of the substantive issues; the emotional ones are equally real. On the other hand, taking the emotional heat out of the situ-ation may not be enough to help people deal with the sub-stantive issues.

/*Two approaches to conflict.* There are two strategies for dealing with conflict in a team or between teams. *Control strategies* can prevent conflict flaring up or can hold things steady while attempts are made to resolve the conflict using *confrontation.* Various control strategies are set out in Table 5.3.

These strategies are what might be called 'smoothing'. Filley (1975, pp. 30—3), in a review of the research on conflict resolution in organisations, identifies four other approaches: withdrawal (avoiding conflict by leaving the organisation), forcing (the use of power to impose a resolution), compromise (seeking a mid-way point, whatever the requirements) and confrontation (putting the two parties together to sort out disputes). Research by Lawrence and Lorsch (1967) concluded that the most successful organisations in terms of their results used more confrontation. Their research shows that successful *and* unsuccessful managers most often use confrontation to resolve disputes, but the successful ones most often use smoothing and compromise alongside it, while unsuccessful managers used forcing and withdrawal alongside it. Control strategies, then, are a useful part dealing with conflict, and are better than using power or running away from disputes, but work best alongside confrontation.

'Confrontation refers to the process in which the parties directly engage each other and focus on the conflict between them' (Walton, 1969, p. 95). *Confrontation strategies* should

Table 5.3 *Avoiding conflict: control strategies*

Strategy	Possible actions	Examples
Avoidance	Avoid situations where disputes arose; reduce triggering events; cooling-off periods	Reduce meetings between parties; set up new system for dealing with conflict subjects; adjourn meetings
Alteration	Change the form or place of the conflict	Agree not to argue in front of others; agree not to criticise each other without making a positive suggestion; meet before conflict situations to resolve problems
Feedback	Explain to parties how others are affected	Other people are upset; team is losing resources; loss of dignity
Help with consequences	Provide support, more rest and thinking time	Neutral person to listen to stressed parties; time off; more social events; encourage getting away from office in lunch time; discourage overwork

be carefully planned. First, the parties should feel similarly about the need to resolve the problems, otherwise one who is unconcerned by the dispute may feel rushed into a confrontation. Second, balancing interpersonal power in the ways that I have suggested puts people on an equal footing during confrontation. Third, situations in which confrontation can occur are found at times when the motivation to confront is highest. Control strategies, ensuring that the first overtures are positive ones in the enquiry mode, and ensuring that positive overtures are reciprocated in like manner, can all help in this. The fourth stage involves two processes. The parties first describe the issues as they understand them and how they feel; they then discuss the similarities between them, acknowledge any common goals, express mutual respect and liking and find positive actions they can share. The two

processes are not necessarily separated, but fairly full exploration of the dispute before agreements are encouraged
increases the scope for full agreement, which Walton says is
based on understanding of the problem. Obviously these
meetings are crucial. Some other helpful ideas for managing
them are to deal with business and substantive issues before
personal and emotional ones; to start with a full exploration
of what has happened in the past, before worrying too much
about resolving present problems and moving forward; to
start with simple social groupings rather than having a mass
meeting of all concerned; and to start in the work setting
rather than an informal setting, e.g. the pub or staff room,
because this puts the affair on a business footing and helps
people feel that personal factors are less of an issue.

During these processes, other members of the team, most
often the leader, and outside consultants can help, by promoting the idea that openness is acceptable, that the feelings and
issues are important and by offering skills and support. Everyone concerned can also help by making the communication
more accurate in the ways discussed earlier in this chapter.
Finally, they can help to keep up the pressure for a resolution,
since if there is not much stress on the parties to the dispute,
they will not suffer the pain of a confrontation, but if they
are unsupported the stress of confrontation may be too much.

Problems with role and work flow have been discussed in
Chapter 4, as well in the earlier parts of this chapter, so they
are not dealt with here.

Sharing work

The final section of this chapter is about sharing work. I have
said frequently that work sharing is an option available to
social workers dealing with problems of teamwork, and to
teams trying to improve their joint activities. There is, however, a major objection to sharing, which is that it may
confuse the client, who may not understand the role of
different workers. This is often a criticism of specialism in
medical settings, for example. Two points can be made in
reply to this. The first is that shared work where both workers
are evidently working together and discuss their sharing with

the client is much less confusing than divided work where advance decisions about areas of responsibility are perhaps inflexibly imposed. Second, explanation to the client is necessary, and the clear definition of roles and tasks in collaborative teamwork makes this easier than in a more conventional structure. It is useful, however, to be able to identify the kind of sharing being used.[1]

Sharing work involves activities at a number of different levels, and understanding these can help teams demonstrate how they are working to clients. Table 5.4 sets out some of these. Each level must include all those at lower levels; it is not possible to undertake joint work effectively unless all the other activities are present. Progression through them, over a period of time, sometimes occurs as a team becomes more used to sharing, but this is not really necessary. It is quite possible to decide one day to work jointly with someone on a case or project, and use all these levels for sharing. Many projects have found that assessment of new cases forms a good basis for starting sharing.

Table 5.4 *Levels of sharing*

Responsive	Alert to the needs of others and their requests for help/support/information
Open	Ready to offer help/support/information where it may be needed
Exchange	Prepared to exchange help/support/information with others even without direct immediate benefits
Planning	Future activities are planned jointly, but implemented separately (planning is separated again if disagreements arise)
Co-ordination	Activities and plans are altered, so that objectives, methods or assumptions are related
Collaboration	Work is divided between two or more team members in defined ways, but carried out separately
Joint work	Work is carried out by team members simultaneously in the same place, in each other's presence

For the individual who wants to share more with others in his team, demonstrating greater responsiveness, openness and willingness to exchange can be a useful way of starting off the process of sharing. As sharing develops in a team where these attitudes are present, it may be better to find work which involves planning or co-ordination, rather than collaborative or joint work, which may come unstuck if attempted without a firm base of experience in lower-level sharing. A team member who is working jointly may find it useful to check whether the relationships between the sharers do include the different kinds of sharing mentioned here — if not, they may be missing an important part of their work and this may lead to later difficulties. Of course, as part of their sharing social workers may have to examine the various different aspects of relating to other members of their teams which I have looked at earlier in this chapter.

Individuals and positions. So far, I have been discussing the relationships between individuals in teams as though all such relationships, and all roles in a team structure, are similar. In general terms this is more or less true, but the positions which individuals hold in a team affect relationships, and so the next chapter looks at some important roles in a team, and their effects on the team and team members.

6

Special Roles in the Team

This chapter looks at the consequences, for individuals and teams, of special roles in a team. There is first a brief discussion of the concept of designation. Then the significant role of team leader is considered at length, followed by briefer discussions of specialist, clerical and administrative, non-professional and outposted staff.

Why designation is important

Designation is the process by which a cluster of tasks, integrated into a role, becomes accepted as having an existence apart from the present incumbent of the role. In a totally collaborative team, tasks would cluster into roles around the particular people taking on the tasks; as they left, the tasks would recluster into new roles. In most teams, however, roles are accepted as continuing, or as valid roles, even if they are discontinued, independent of the individuals involved. Designation occurs in two basic ways with many variants. One way is that the agency designates some roles, e.g. leader, secretary, specialist, social worker, assistant. The other way is that roles are formed in a team and considered to have independent validity as a result of how the team works. Designation has an element of formality, either by official act, or explicit recognition through some process internal to the team.

Three aspects of designation are important. First, it provides an element of certainty and continuity in what would otherwise be a flexible and insecure group. Second, it confirms the importance of some aspects of the work of the team. Third, it is an essential part of clarifying the power structure of a team, because it allocates certain kinds of power and responsibility to particular roles, and designation signifies that the people occupying these roles are accepted as users of the rewards, sanctions, respect, etc., associated with that power.

Understanding designation is helpful in reducing conflicts about who designated whom and how. Designation is also a central factor in team leadership, because the term 'leader' is often used in two ways — one who has the ability to be a leader, and one who is a designated leader. Designation, since it offers various powers, often supports someone in using his leadership abilities; having good ability often reinforces a designated leader. In this book I reserve the term 'leader' to someone who is designated as such.

The remainder of this chapter is concerned with various roles whose designation in social work teams is common, but which sometimes arouses difficulty either for the incumbents or other team members.

The team leader

Most teams have a designated leader. Established teams in agencies usually have an officially designated one, and in groups working with individual cases or groups of clients a leader is often informally or formally designated, or one member is assumed to be the leader. The existence of leaders can result in an assumption that the team is leader-centred and communication is centralised, even though a collaborative style might be possible. Formal designation may also conflict with informal ideas about who should be the leader, so there may be conflict surrounding who has influence in designation and how it occurs.

Ideas about leadership

Before discussing practicalities, it is useful to look at the ideas which exist about leadership. This brief discussion is based on the summaries of Ribeaux and Poppleton (1978) and Fraser (1978b). There has been a debate about whether leaders are born or made by circumstances, and this led to much research on the characteristics of leaders. Stogdill (1948) surveyed many studies and comments as follows:

> The findings suggest that leadership is not a matter of passive status, or of the mere possession of some combination of traits. It appears rather to be a working relationship among members of a group, in which the leader acquires status through active participation and demonstration of his capacity for carrying co-operative tasks through to completion. Significant aspects of this capacity for organising and expediting co-operative effort appear to be intelligence, alertness to the needs and motives of others, and insight into situations, further reinforced by such habits as responsibility, initiative, persistence and self-confidence (Stogdill, in Gibb, 1969, p. 127).

Later studies have led to a move towards situational (Vroom and Yetton, 1973) and contingency (Fiedler, 1969) approaches to leadership. In essence these suggest that circumstances limit the ways in which leaders can behave, and that they can vary the way they lead according to the situation they find themselves in. There is empirical research in industrial and commercial settings which reinforces the validity of these ideas.

One practically useful analysis is by Vroom and Yetton (1973), who identified five leadership styles in groups. These are autocratic (A1 — you decide on your own using your existing information; A2 — you get subordinates to find the information you want, then you make the decision); consultative (C1 — you get ideas from subordinates individually, then make the decision; C2 — you explore it with them as a group, then you make the decision); or group (you share the problem with the group, discuss alternatives and try to reach consensus, and the consensus is accepted).

It is suggested that managers look at the situation they are faced with and ask themselves how much group support they need in the circumstances, whether, if they seek it, the team

is likely to be operating on a basis which accepts the fundamental policies of the agency, and if group decision-making
is needed to prevent conflict in the team. Having made this
assessment, managers can decide which style of leadership
they should use.

Studies have shown that experienced managers use the
leadership styles suggested by the research in about two-thirds
of cases; the rules protecting group acceptance were the most
often broken in the other third. This is something of a warn-
ing: leaders should make sure they get team support if they
need it. There is evidence that managers are able to move
between these styles and take into account the situational
factors involved (Ribeaux and Poppleton, 1978, p. 292). ↑

Team leadership in social work

To sum up the variety of ideas covered in the last section,
I have presented a leader as someone who organises co-
operation in a group by paying attention to defining tasks
and situations and the needs of others, and varying the way
in which power attached to designated leadership is used
according to the situation. Since teams are relatively small
groups of people, the capacity to work with group processes
is more important than pedagogic or demagogic powers
which might be useful for teacher and politician leaders.

↑ There are a number of useful ideas about leadership which
are relevant in practice. The first is that the leader should be
open to influence. This is because

> the amount of influence a leader can actually have over
> team members is determined by how much the group is
> allowed to influence the leader. *The interesting thing is
> that the team members are not gaining influence at the
> expense of the leader.* There is simply much more influ-
> ence being exerted (Ends and Page, 1977, p. 61, emphasis
> in original).

This idea is Likert's (1961) principle of interaction influence. If team members are allowed to influence the leader's

decisions, they will have more commitment to these decisions, and so he will have more influence over their subsequent actions, though this can only work if there is no fundamental difference of policy or principle.

The second point about practical leadership is that a leader should arrange the *equal availability of knowledge* so that team members can trust that the leader is keeping them in touch with the wider organisation. This involves questions of judgement, however. Passing on everything can be just as obstructive as limiting information if team members cannot deal with the quantity offered. Team leaders, however, do not have to pass everything on verbally, or at meetings, or be totally responsible for communication. All team members can be responsible for part of the information coming to the team, and for supplying it to others as needed. |

| The third function of leaders is to provide a *place and time for discussion* which reflects this openness and equality. General or specific team meetings should encourage and permit all kinds of contribution. All the team can help, but leaders must ensure that everyone is enabled to contribute (see pp. 59—60 for a brief discussion of team meetings).

The fourth leadership requirement is that individuals' contributions must be *valued and effective,* even if the leader or members of the team eventually reject them. Influence is no good unless it works, so leaders should work hard demonstrably to show the team that their ideas are taken seriously. One or two failures soon lead to disillusionment with teamwork. Reasons for failure should be clearly understood by the team.

All these issues relate to an important aspect of leadership: *dealing with distrust.* All people with designated statuses, even those without power, are distrusted by others. Team leaders are often distrusted either because team members are not sure whether they can get what the team wants, or because team members think the designated status may be used against them.|An individual who does things for another person runs the risk that the other might think he or she could have done better, especially when things go wrong. Dealing with distrust requires awareness and openness. Analysing the likely outcome of activities undertaken on behalf of the team and warning members of the likelihood of success may reduce distrust. It may be possible to involve the team in the activity, so that their skill as well as the leader's has influence. For example, the staff in a home for the mentally ill in an SSD decided to try to get the admission procedure changed, so the warden (i.e. team leader) sought policy changes in the SSD. Several managers in the residential section of the SSD were opposed, she discussed this with her team, and one member suggested that they should try to get support in the fieldwork section to influence the residential section. They all approached colleagues, and a committee on the use of the hostel resulted in which the team were able to argue their case — although not completely successfully. This example also demonstrates openness to influence, and valuing team members' contributions.

In any situation the leader has a *responsibility to start things going*. While any member of a team can start new activities or ideas, the leader should review the team's activities constantly to see if it is taking up its opportunities, and do something if it is not.

It follows that leaders should *ensure that the group process is considered* by the team, even if they do not always take a lead in this.

Finally, team leaders should take responsibility for the *efficiency of the systems* used by the team — again not necessarily by setting up the systems, but by ensuring that it is done in a collaborative team. Where relationships and accountability are fluid, it is easy for things to get lost; so administrative support, records and decision-making systems must be impeccable, but not obtrude upon people's equal involvement.

Leadership problems

The major problem for a team leader in doing all this comes from *sharing responsibility*. Different patterns of teamwork involve more or less sharing of responsibility, so this may not be a problem. Where it is, in collaborative teamwork, I argued earlier (pp. 13—16) that it is not insurmountable. If there is a system of roles which meets the clients' needs, a structure for deciding priorities and other problems, and clear task divisions in individual work, much of the team leaders' responsibility to the organisation has been accepted.

The second problem of team leadership is *negotiation* in the opposite direction: representing the needs of the team's clients to the organisation. In many social work agencies the team leader negotiates the agency's policy with the team, altering it to fit clients' needs, and influencing the policy by pressing those needs on the agency. The agency's policy derives from broad-range policies originated for a wide population by powerful opinion-formers in society, and sometimes does not suit a particular community's or client group's needs, which in turn provides a powerful base for team members' views of desirable social policy. The team leader is in the middle of these powerful positions, and negotiates between them.

Various possibilities are open in such negotiations. Leaders can look for principles or policies in the agency's approach or the community's needs which override more detailed administrative instructions or short-term needs. Inconsistencies between the policies or views of the agency or team members, and between their general policies and particular practice, practical considerations, ethical issues or staff and personnel matters can be used in arguments. |

For example, one SSD area team's superiors had decided that a group for single parents with school-age children would not be provided because the department had higher priorities, especially child abuse. In response the team collected information that the area had a higher-than-average proportion of single-parent families, producing a higher-than-average proportion of deprived and at-risk children. They argued that meeting the community's particular needs would attack longer-term problems better than a policy of concentrating on younger children. Eventually, permission, although not finance, was given for the group.

Leadership in different kinds of team

| So far I have discussed some general aspects of leadership. These can be applied in different ways depending on the

leader's and team's preference and the agency's needs. In Table 6.1 I have set out applications of the main aspects of leadership in each of three common types of team: collaborative, individualised and leader-centred teams. Leaders and teams may find it useful to work through the possibilities to assess what setting their leadership style approximates to, and to get ideas for changes which might be possible.

Specialist roles

Specialisation is a confusing issue (see Payne, 1979, for a longer discussion of the problems of the concept). It may

Table 6.1   *Variations in leadership style*

Characteristics of leadership	Team types		
	Collaborative (shared responsibility)	Individualistic (equally skilled workers take personal responsibility for their work)	Leader-centred (less-skilled workers are responsible to leader)
Openness to influence	Promotes situations where members can influence leader, who responds to such influence	Accepts members' judgements as equally valid with leader's and responds to their views	Prepared to listen to members' views and amend leader's views if this seems appropriate
Equal availability of knowledge	Promotes systems so that all members can join in gaining and using information	Encourages team members to seek specialist knowledge and passes on relevant material to the appropriate member	Sets up a system so that members can find information they need, and readily shares leader's own knowledge and skills
Place and time for discussion	Promotes equal participation by all members in meetings and decision-making structures	Ensures that team members have a chance to raise matters of joint relevance with others	Ensures regular meetings which cover the main issues of concern to members, and allows members to raise issues at these meetings
Contributions valued and effective	Promotes enquiry mode and genuine respect for all members' work and values	Makes clear that members' work is valued, and supports their ideas and projects	Accepts that all members contribute, praises good contributions, supports further developments actively
Dealing with distrust	Leader's actions often explained, examined and justified in public, leader accepts and responds helpfully to signs of distrust	Leader explains actions if others criticise	Leader is alert to feelings of distrust and explains actions and events if these arise
Responsibility to start things going	Constantly raises chances for change or action with the whole team	Suggests possible developments to members most concerned	Plays a leading role in taking forward ideas for projects, actively takes part in projects started by members
Ensuring that group processes are considered	Raises in the enquiry mode with the team issues and interpretations about group processes	Raises problems with the individuals concerned	Takes action to adjust group processes where there are difficulties
Efficient systems	Discusses with team and implements decisions where inefficiency is found by members	Raises problems with individuals concerned and supports attempts to find solutions	Takes action to resolve administrative difficulties and explains actions or consults team

mean that specialists' responsibilities might be limited to their specialism, or that most of their work might be within it, or that a specialist just knows a lot more than most about the subject. Specialisation can mean that specialists are recognisably more skilful or more able in their area than others. Or it can just mean that specialists work in *different* areas, not necessarily more skilfully. Specialisation can be based on many factors, but in teams it is useful to look at three. *Domain* specialisation occurs where the subject-matter of work (e.g. client group) is the basis of specialisation. *Task* specialisation is based on particular skills and activities. *Role* specialisation is based on the position occupied in the team (e.g. intake worker, home help). Specialisation is strongest when all three of these go together. For example, welfare rights officers employed by some SSDs have a domain in welfare rights work, where information is difficult for a non-specialist to maintain; they work on the task of advocay using skills and knowledge which are infrequently used by others; and they have a defined role independent of normal team functioning. Specialist workers with the elderly in SSDs are in the opposite position. Others can quickly acquire the necessary knowledge of the elderly, so there is a less strong domain. The tasks involved are within the range of most social workers, whose skills can transfer without difficulty to this client group. There is rarely an explicit role for specialists in such work; they are ordinary members of the generic team.

This discussion emphasises the idea of exclusivity in most people's assumptions and definitions of a specialist. Exclusivity implies status, and status problems are one of the difficulties for a designated specialist in an otherwise equal team, where the specialist may, aside from his specialism, also be of equal status. It is sometimes difficult to deal with lower-status staff who possess some characteristics of the specialist. For example, a social work assistant in an SSD who deals with nearly all work with the elderly is a specialist in the sense that his/her domain is different, but is of lower hierarchical status and is theoretically less skillful than a generic social worker. The fact that his/her domain is different seems to imply greater skill or exclusivity which either does not exist or is not normally recognised in status terms.

Concentrating on dealing with exclusivity, whether actual or perceived, can help to deal with the problems of specialisation. Specialists can openly offer their knowledge and expertise. Consultation, for instance, involves others in the domain, while maintaining the specialism and high-quality services. Working in the other direction, non-specialists can make their interest in a specialist domain clear and ask to share work or consult the specialist. Arguments in support of this are that it provides continuity and alternative sources of expertise if the specialist leaves or is absent, and it develops expertise in the team. Teams may also have to consider designating more than one specialist in each domain.

Sometimes team members do not accept their informally designated expertise or difference (this seems to be common in SSD teams — see DHSS, 1978) or seek designation or are designated as expert when they are merely different. Discussing work flow can be an unthreatening way of raising this (e.g. 'Dave seems to be getting a lot of work with the elderly. Are we intentionally making him a specialist, or is he not getting a fair proportion of other work?').

Finally, specialists need to be aware of boundary problems (see pp. 67–8). Because their specialism is a way of defining domains, and they have to maintain the boundaries, they should watch for cases where another way of defining domains is better, and be prepared to relax their boundaries.

Clerical and administrative staff

Clerical and administrative staff (and often other non-social workers) present a problem in teamwork for many social work agencies. They always exist, they are essential to the work, but are they part of the team? This is more complicated in agencies where clerical staff are responsible to managers of administrative services rather than or as well as to staff who work with clients. Separating responsibility like this creates uncertainty.

Clerical staff (e.g. telephonists, receptionists) do a considerable amount of work with clients. Hall (1975a) shows that receptionists have influence over how or whether clients are dealt with. Also, smooth administration is essential to efficient service, and clerical staff as well as social workers may be better motivated if they participate in team decisions. Many writers describing teamwork regard involving clerical staff in the work group as essential in creating good teamwork for these reasons. Unless they are involved, there can be misunderstanding or hostility to other team members' work or confusion about flexible roles in a collaborative team. On the other hand, administrative staff are often bored in general staff meetings where they feel that things being discussed have no relevance for them.

It is important therefore to work out how clerical staff should be involved in team decisions, and have this generally agreed. A variety of team meetings for different purposes may be the answer (see pp. 59–60). Recognition of clerical staff training, and of social and career needs can help. So also can attention to the geography of the office, so that clerical staff are neither isolated nor interrupted.

Non-professional staff

In Chapter 2 I discussed some policy debates about using non-professionals in the social services. The practical implications of involving such people in teams are neatly summed up by Kane (1980, p. 142), in her survey of research into multi-disciplinary teams:

> When professionals were included as full-fledged team members, the team was more likely to adhere to an integrative [collaborative] pattern; one would be hard put, however, to decide whether the presence of para-professionals of various disciplines led to a change in pattern or whether those with the integrative format were more likely to be able to include para-professionals in their deliberations.

Where non-professionals are employed and actively involved in teamwork, then, there is a move towards collaborative work either through the effort of involving non-professionals or because involving non-professionals in decisions only happens in a collaborative team.

If the latter is the case, why should this be? Possible factors might be the low status of the non-professional in matters of salary and qualifications; a low regard for the skills employed in their work and a perception that their roles are a hived-off part of the functions of professionals rather than constituting a whole contribution to the agency. In non-collaborative teams official designation is so important that non-professionals find it difficult to avoid conventional assumptions about their role.

Finally, perhaps in non-collaborative teams, either leader-centred or individualistic, the power structure of the team assumes that inferior team members will accept responsibility and make contributions through superior members who are responsible for their work, rather than on their own account.

Working with and involving non-professional workers may be a strategy for questioning many of these assumptions. Teams which want to do this, either in order to move towards collaborative work, or because they need to involve non-professionals more in their work, have to consider the three groups of issues I have raised, dealing with status problems, decision-making and task definition.

Dealing with status problems

The team may want to compensate for status differences. Active encouragement to non-professionals about the value of their contribution may be helpful. So also is limiting behaviour in the team which devalues such contributions. Important contributions from non-professionals are their local origins and similar background to many clients, unlike some social workers. Non-professionals may be more likely to share and respond to the interests, accent and priorities of local people than an outside professional, to interpret these to the team, and relate better and more quickly to clients, especially where differences are considerable (e.g. ethnic differences). Non-professionals are often in a position where they have much more frequent, regular and practical contact with clients and learn basic information which is useful to others in the team who do not have the length or type of contact with clients to get such knowledge. In general team discussions, and in discussions about individual cases, non-professionals can be called upon for these interpretations and team members can listen to them with respect without devaluing their own skills.

Practical skills and common-sense interpretations unaffected by theoretical ideas are other valuable contributions made by non-professionals. Finally, they are often much more closely in touch with what would be locally politically and socially acceptable as a way of dealing with clients than social workers. On one occasion, for instance, a middle-class volunteer in a probation team warned that the proposed recommendations for community service by two sexual offenders in a children's home would be criticised if it were publicly revealed, and suggested an old people's home instead. The team resisted this on the grounds that there was in fact no cause for concern. She persisted, however, in pointing out the attitudes of others outside the agency, and how these would adversely affect the clients if they became the victims of a public debate, and the proposal was changed. Of course, the change pandered to conventional assumptions, and can be seen as inappropriate, but the volunteer had more understanding of the strength of conventional assumptions in the face of the real facts which supported the professionals' argument, and was eventually able to convince them that she was right, even though they were unhappy about it.

It is often difficult not to devalue the contribution made by non-professionals; they do not make the assumptions, and are often unable to take the short-cuts, that social workers make in discussion, and this can be frustrating to professionals in team discussions. It is useful to follow the practice of accepting all contributions made to discussions as worth while and being clear about how and why an idea finally is rejected or accepted, especially if it comes from a non-professional. Many non-professionals, especially volunteers, are not invited to team or decision-making meetings either because this is inconvenient or someone thinks it is inappropriate. If they are not available at the time of a general meeting, arrangements can be made for them to be involved in decision-making in the agency at another time. In leader-centred teams this might mean a meeting of volunteers with team leaders; in individualistic teams individual workers might consult with volunteers and para-professionals they are responsible for, and in a collaborative team a representative meeting may solve this problem. In teams dealing with individual cases, projects or institutions, non-professionals can be involved as equal staff members in all meetings concerned with their clients or responsibilities. Sometimes, the non-professional may not take up such involvement, especially if it is time-consuming, but feels valued if the chance is there.

Decision-making

This leads me on to the problems of involving non-professionals in decisions about individual cases. Many of the general aspects of reducing status differences apply equally here. Additionally, social workers sharing work with non-professionals can involve them in decision-making in a number of other ways.

First, regular, set meetings to exchange information rather than *ad hoc* arrangements provide more security for the non-professional. Shared work with the client can help stimulate this. Second, planning the work can be done jointly, rather than with the social worker delegating tasks to the non-professional. This increases commitment and clear task and role definitions. Third, non-professionals can be involved in decision-making meetings in the agency (e.g. reviews, meetings to decide about admission to residential homes) or outside it (e.g. court hearings). Even if they cannot attend, they can brief the social worker with their views and information, and the social worker can report back on events later. Non-professionals involved in a meeting with other professionals should be briefed about the nature of the meeting, their role and the roles of others, so that they can feel confident enough to make useful contributions, even to decisions (e.g. reception into care) which must finally be made by professionals.

A good deal of evidence and experience suggests that this can be especially helpful in creating an environment in residential and day-care settings which helps clients to progress in their treatment and in reducing institutionalisation. In many such settings, however, treatment planning is often done by senior or external staff and is not passed on to staff in daily contact with residents, who are 'only' doing routine caring. In the process of that work, however, they learn much which can benefit decision-making, and they can obstruct or help treatment considerably.

Task definition

Task definition is very little different for non-professionals than for professionals, because there are no categories of tasks which can always be allocated to non-professionals. Careful assessment is needed of the most appropriate person for particular tasks, professional or not, bearing in mind their levels of skills (see pp. 50—3).

Supervising non-professionals

Many social workers find supervising non-professionals' work a difficult task. Supervision is not generally a part of an ordinary social worker's role. Even in residential or day care, where the management of a large non-professional staff is a normal part of the professional's role, professional *supervision* is not a common activity. Also, the conventional style of social work supervision is not always appropriate for non-professionals, being directed to broadening the social worker's capacity for independent action in a wide range of activities. Non-professionals, on the other hand, need help in carrying out specific tasks in particular situations, and it is helpful if supervision is more clearly focused on defining and planning what is to be done in individual cases, and identifying the non-professional's skills and experience which enable him to help.

Thigpen (1979) carried out research in the USA into the

kind of behaviour which inexperienced para-professionals and supervisors found most helpful, and his findings seem realistically applicable to the United Kingdom. He found that supervisors were most helpful if they *made time* to discuss things with the non-professional and seemed *approachable*; if they showed *concern for* the non-professional's *feelings, respect* for their views and *confidence* in their work; if the skills and competence of the supervisor allowed the non-professional to use the former as *a role model*; if the supervisor ensured that the *organisation and systems* of the agency efficiently *supported* the non-professional's work; if the supervisor concentrated on *discussing the client's problems and ways of dealing with them*, rather than broad strategies and methods; if the supervisor provided *specific feedback* to the non-professional on the things he has done well or badly, rather than on his judgement, personality or awareness; and if the supervisor helped the non-professional develop *new skills and responsibilities*. The most important factors seemed to be respecting and valuing the non-professional's views and work, and concentrating on specifics in feedback rather than generalities or non-professionals' personality. It appeared that supervisors did not realise how important their position as a role model to non-professionals was. As non-professionals gain experience, of course, a broader, less specific supervision style may be more appropriate. Thigpen's study does provide support, however, for a fairly specific style of supervision.

Developing non-professional work

Growth in the use of non-professionals has come about in three ways. First, existing non-professionals have been more involved in decision-making and more valued for the contribution they make to an agency's work. In residential homes and in social service agencies care assistants, home helps, ancillaries and assistants have all felt this change in recent years; but many have not yet been involved to the extent that I have discussed here. The second way is in the increase in the use of volunteers and para-professionals, both absolutely and in proportion to the growth of professionals. The third way is in the range of work which it has been recognised that such workers can undertake. The high standard of counselling provided by marriage guidance, citizens advice and samaritan workers demonstrates what could be achieved over a wider field. In social work agencies tasks which were left undone can now be carried out efficiently because larger numbers of non-professionals can be made available to serve clients. In the future the professional worker's role may become the support of groups of non-professionals rather than providing direct casework services, as in the American Midway project (Schwartz and Sample, 1972).

Increasing the use of non-professionals implies all three of these approaches, since it needs a preparedness to broaden the work which is allocated to non-professional workers, which in turn requires a higher proportion of them in the staffing structures of agencies, and this, also, implies greater concern for their involvement. As larger numbers are used and employed, greater concern is needed for their career development. This has led in the USA to planning for career lattices (see Austin, 1978), which have grown from the new careers ideas that it is worth finding ways of employing people who have not gained or cannot gain conventional education which alone allows them to take up professional roles. A variety of different paths is devised through patterns of experience and in-service training which will enable staff to achieve promotion in a hierarchical agency and broaden their responsibilities. The developing structure of social services education in the United Kingdom is moving towards providing such a pattern. The CSS programme of modular courses based on job descriptions of the workers involved (Ash *et al.*, 1980) allows entry to a variety of careers including access to professional CQSW training and through that or directly to post-qualifying training. There are signs in a number of projects that recruiting local para-professional workers is a way of involving people with natural helping skills in formal social service agencies (e.g. the Strathclyde plan to employ, train and offer permanent jobs to unemployed people: Community Care, 1980).

There are many reports of projects involving non-professionals in teamwork in the USA, and descriptions of a variety of programmes in schools, social work agencies, residential settings, mental health community and hospital settings, and various community projects can be found in Gartner (1971), Grosser *et al.* (1969), Riessman and Popper (1968) and Wicks (1978). These writers, together with Austin (1978), give access to many other articles and books covering the subject. Many of them reveal clearly how valuable the effect of greater involvement, greater numbers, greater range and greater opportunities of work with non-professionals is, and how this can have profound effects on the nature of professionals' work, the development of teamwork and many benefits in the service of a wide variety of clients in a wide variety of settings. In the United Kingdom the publications of the Volunteer Centre and accounts of various projects show a similar pattern (e.g. Ager's (1979) account of the use of hospital-based aides to help patients transfer home, and the use of home helps with the mentally disordered, Payne (1977)).

Outposted staff

The difficult role of outposted staff is particularly important in teamwork, because outposting is often used to enhance collaboration between organisations or parts of organisations. Outposting occurs when a worker who is part of one work group is placed in another group in order either to bring some expertise normally contained in the first group into the second, or to build relationships between the two groups. Outposted workers are usually in a minority in the receiving group, have a different specialism in some way, and are responsible within two different organisational structures. They may (but not necessarily) form part of a matrix structure. Outposting may involve permanent attachment to another organisation, temporary attachment for a particular task, or intermittent association for liaison and for some of the worker's activities to be performed in the organisation of origin and some in the outpost. A number of questions arise for outposted workers.

Loyalty

First, they may be expected to retain loyalties to two different groups, which may possess different ideologies or assumptions. They can be helped to deal with this problem before outposting takes place by attempts on both sides to define where assumptions are similar, different but not in conflict, and in conflict. Often, however, outposted workers are left to sort out these problems as they go along. If this happens, making it explicit when problems arise, and reporting both conflicts *and similarities* to both sides on a regular basis, might help. An external consultant, or someone with the same professional background to discuss the conflicts and strengthen the outposted worker's independence, is helpful.

Knowledge

Outposted workers may have a problem in keeping up with information within and about both groups. They may not have the time to attend relevant meetings in both settings, or absorb paperwork from both, or maintain an interest in relevant professional developments. Even if this is possible, aligning conflicts of views and practice may be difficult, and the information from both settings may be inappropriate for someone on the boundaries of both. Teams can help in this by taking special account in their work of the position of outposted staff, by setting up channels for passing information and by being prepared to repeat information for outposted colleagues who have not picked it up.

Position

The special position of being a go-between also raises problems. Outposted workers may be trusted by neither side, and so may come to lean towards one or the other; physical provision (e.g. desks, telephones) may be unsatisfactory because such workers are marginal in both organisations; and their powers and responsibilities may be circumscribed at either or both ends and others who are involved do not realise that this is happening. Again, clarity and care are needed to work out these difficulties.

The advantages of outposting

In spite of the problems outposting can be a way of overcoming boundary problems. Intermittent or temporary outposting can be useful in building up a relationship between a field team and a residential home, a probation office and a prison, a casework team and a local community project. It is particularly valuable where clients are moved backwards and forwards across the boundary, so that continuity of service can be maintained, or where several professional groups ought to be involved in service to a client, in which case providing it in one setting using outposted professionals from elsewhere is a useful strategy. So, outposting is a way of fitting divided organisations and professions and their services to the whole needs of a client, and I shall discuss it further, together with other strategies for bridging the gap between teams and their organisational and professional contexts, in the next chapter.

7

The Team and its Context

This chapter discusses how teams can fit in with influences from the context within which they work. The first part looks at the professional context by considering multi-disciplinary teamwork, while the second looks at the organisational context of teamwork.

Multi-disciplinary teams: extra dimensions to teamwork

In most respects multi-disciplinary teams are no different from any other kind of team. The purpose of this section is to identify those aspects of such teams which present additional problems.

There are three extra dimensions to multi-disciplinary teamwork. First, multi-disciplinary teams consist of *different occupational groups* which are usually regarded as having autonomy from one another, and the team is set up to enable them to co-operate better, usually because they have co-operated badly before. Members of different occupational groups are trained and socialised into their groups, and often use rather different theoretical and knowledge bases (so that multi-disciplinary teams are often also inter disciplinary, by which I mean that they combine different fields of learning).

To deal with these problems requires careful attention to what each person brings to the team (see Table 5.1 and pp. 62—6). Most writers argue that domain- and role-blurring is inappropriate in a multi-disciplinary team (e.g. Wright, 1978), and the appropriate way of co-operating is to keep the ideals of the occupational group as a reference point and negotiate on tasks and boundaries (Hiltner, 1958). Sometimes a loose network of workers coming together for specific tasks is more appropriate than creating a collaborative team (Hey, 1979). If a team is being developed, using ideas like those presented in Chapter 4, the process of development might rely therefore more on Lamberts and Riphagen's (1975) model of defining and aligning boundaries and reducing unrealistic stereotypes than Brill's (1976) group-process development model. Involvement in a multi-disciplinary team requires of members that they have a very strong idea of their own occupational role, can explain it, and demonstrate its practice well (Cockerill, 1953). It is important to understand clearly the roles of the other groups involved.

Second, we have to consider the *organisational aspects* of multi-disciplinary teams. Often they are set up alongside attempts to co-ordinate the work of different agencies, each of which has a dominant occupational group. This means that occupational differences are emphasised in organisational divisions and organisational problems are reflected in, or even unrealistically blamed upon, multi-disciplinary teamwork, or the lack of it, so careful organisational support to multi-disciplinary work should be recruited. A variety of alternative possibilities in the health and social services are equally viable, depending on the arrangement of resources, and administratively it is difficult to decide which is best, or even to control planning and resource provision. Different groups of workers will be responsible through hierarchies in different organisations or occupational groups. A matrix hierarchy (p. 22) may help to resolve this, and team members can argue that this reduces time-wasting at every level, eases policy-making, and from their point of view speeds decision-making and makes it more relevant to their needs and more co-ordinated than seeking decisions with different hierarchies.

If multi-disciplinary teams have to work through different hierarchies, timing is important, and the team should try to ensure that requests for decisions are made early enough in all organisations and in any necessary sequence (e.g. go to social services committee for approval, then housing committee). Another possibility is to ask both organisations to take the decision simultaneously, but make each decision dependent upon the other. Different forms of presentation can be made to each organisation, but they should be consistent, because this is often checked. Finally, matters which might raise personal or professional hackles should be avoided, because these can demolish or obstruct otherwise reasonable proposals. Anything which may change an individual's or organisation's power, status or boundaries may produce problems. A hidden status issue sometimes arises if an otherwise reasonable proposal attacks a profession's assumption that it alone should decide the point. For example, doctors react badly to anything which suggests that they are not alone responsible for deciding treatment for their patients, so suggesting that others should be involved in such decisions can provoke rejection. Teachers feel similarly about curricula, and this sometimes causes problems in assessment centres or community schools run by SSDs which include teaching staff.

Third, multi-disciplinary teams obviously pose problems of *status and leadership*. Any team with a doctor in it tends towards a leader-centred pattern with the doctor as leader (Kane, 1980, p. 143): because others are used to a subordinate position and the group process reflects this (Odhner, 1970, p. 487); because doctors are either employed as independent contractors rather than employees, or are legally responsible for decisions about their patients and therefore resist the involvement of others; and also because they are usually men, and the other occupational groups around them are often women, so gender and class status backs up their dominance (McIntosh and Dingwall, 1978, p. 120). Status problems exist also where there is *uncertainty* about status, or where the basis for it might be *disputed*. It is unclear, for instance, whether teachers, nurses, psychologists and social workers have broadly equivalent statuses. Different people value these jobs differently. The nurse's caring role tends to be highly valued, the social worker's less well understood. The medical and academic knowledge base of nursing and teaching is accepted, the sociological knowledge base of social work less so. On the other hand, social workers are often rather better paid and more independent than many nurses. All this can lead to uncertainties and conflicts in multi-disciplinary teams.

Two different strategies can help in dealing with status and leadership problems. If they are accepted, or high-status leaders can be persuaded to join in, general reviews of teamwork, team-building, concentrating on task and role definition, or work on leadership may bring results. Less formally, regular explanation of a team member's own task and how he/she sees the work may improve clarity. The alternative is to define the role of team members who do not want to be involved in collaborative work and work jointly with others, referring work to the non-collaborators as required. This is often done with doctors, who in effect 'prescribe' treatment by the rest of the team in the same way that they prescribe medicine, and have medical problems referred back to them. In all multi-disciplinary teamwork, however, it is likely that regular association works better than intermittent liaison. In primary health care, for example, research by Corney and Briscoe (1977) and Goulstone and Jones (1976) suggests that attachment to family doctor practices has some effect in breaking down hostility and educating health-care professionals, but liaison schemes where social workers only have regular contact from another base do not change patterns of relationships.

Two more general strategies to promoting multi-disciplinary work are significant: consultation and training.

Consultation in multi-disciplinary work

One of the problems raised by many writers about multi-disciplinary work is clients' confusion if they have to relate to more than one worker. One way of dealing with this is through consultation so that a one-worker—one-client service can be given by a team using a variety of different specialist skills channelled through one person. It can also be used to provide specialist skills between people in the same occupational group in a uni-disciplinary team. One misunderstanding that some social workers have is that consultation only applies to more skilled and experienced workers who have superior status giving advice to less experienced workers. This is not so: every worker can give advice and help to others whatever his/her status and experience; we all have skills which others may wish to rely on.

The following two case studies show such consultation at work in two different settings, and draw together many of my other comments on multi-disciplinary work. They both show the importance of setting up a clear system for collaboration in a multi-disciplinary team, the clear differentiation of tasks in the particular case along the lines of previously identified roles for each different worker, and respect for the values of other occupational groups. The first looks at a project in a multi-disciplinary child-guidance team to create teamwork between social workers and staff in schools through consultancy.

* * *

The schools consultancy project: by Renee Daines

Avon Child Guidance Service decided that they should take a more continuing responsibility for children who had gone to special schools largely on their recommendation. This was one of the reasons for changing my role from being a member of a multi-disciplinary team working in a child-guidance clinic to that of a social worker with a special responsibility for work with three special schools from a child-guidance base. Although in theory the home child-guidance team kept up links between child, family and school and they continued to work with the family in order to change the home situation while the child was away, once the crisis of the child's behaviour was resolved with the special school placement, the case took less priority in a busy clinic's time. Work was often limited to reviews at holiday periods, and further decisions about placement, if changes were needed. We hoped that giving one social worker special responsibility for these children would reduce the problems caused for schools and parents of this relative neglect.

The schools were all very different. School *A* was a residential community in the heart of the country, seventy miles from Bristol. It took about thirty children aged 8–12 who were defined as 'maladjusted'; it had a slight bias towards 'delicate' children and tended to take a number of these whose emotional problems seemed to stem from physical difficulties (e.g. asthmatics). School *B* was a day school for emotionally disturbed children who were brought by taxi from all over the city. There was a wide age range of children who had proved impossible to manage in ordinary schools. School *C* was a day school for mildly subnormal children aged 13-plus, where there was a new head teacher and the child-guidance service wanted to build up contacts.

I rapidly felt superfluous in school *C* as I appeared to be intervening to prevent rather than facilitate local clinic contacts and so I phased myself out fairly soon. In the other two schools I tried to fill a mixed role. We arranged for a team, drawn from several clinic teams, of child psychiatrist, educational psychologist and myself to visit fortnightly for a meeting with all school staff on a consultative basis. This was intended to provide a background organisation from which more individualised consultation could be planned. There was an uneasy mix of general case discussion and consultation at the meetings, in which the consultative team wanted to help the head and other teachers look at their own skills in managing disturbed children.

In school *A* this move was welcomed by the head, who came from an authority which offered a lot of psychiatric support, and who wanted, I think, to educate his staff. The teachers were mainly concerned to discuss individual children. With hindsight, this difference in aims was not very clear, and we often fell to discussing particular children with a will, in order to avoid more difficult general discussion about handling children's behaviour in school. The consultative team had their mutual relationships and roles well established through previous contact, and we failed because of this to be clear about what we were doing with the school staff. In school *B* I was part of a different and less well-established team trying to fulfil the same role. Here, the school staff were much more divided on how they saw their own role and there were evident feelings of rivalry and competition between the child-guidance team and head teacher, and the school staff. Because of this, it proved much more difficult to establish a consistent role for the team.

Individually, however, there was more success, since I also

attempted in this school to work with several of the children's families, and in one case worked also with a teenage girl within the school. More commonly, the child psychiatrist would see the child at school, and we would seek occasional informal case conferences in which we influenced the way in which both of us worked. Although this is the conventional child-guidance model of work, in which social workers deal mainly with parents and psychiatrists with the children, the clinic background was not available, but the regular meetings with the school staff provided the background of working together which supported our individual work.

How did this collection of disparate team memberships work? It felt a bit like 'jack of all trades and master of none'. My expertise was under threat; I had no secure niche; I was unsure of my role, doubtful of its validity and anxious about how it could be implemented. The well-established team support of clinic membership was replaced by several different and much more ephemeral support systems. The feelings of isolation I at times experienced were unexpected and reinforced for me the importance of at least having a home base.

Specially written for this book by Renee Daines

*   *   *

In the account of this project it seems that relationships and consultative work were much more successful where, in school *A*, there was mutual respect between the groups and the consultative team, and they were clear, if inexplicit, about their own roles within their group. Where respect, as indicated by a willingness to refer to the clinic for social work and other services, was absent, in school *C*, contact broke down very quickly. In school *B* the struggle to make explicit and deal with the misunderstandings and conflicts led, in spite of the difficulties, to individual work. The loss of a traditional role and mutual support clearly made it difficult for the social worker to be sure what her job should be, and the lack of other professional support increased her isolation because of her outposting from a social work or conventional child-guidance setting to an unplanned and constantly changing multi-professional group.

Some of these difficulties are handled more successfully in institutions. The second case study where consultancy was used is in a multi-disciplinary hospital team where different members of staff provide consultancy for one another, even across the usual status lines.

*   *   *

After self-harm, a case study: by Nick Welch

This case is taken from work on the Barnes Unit in Oxford, which is a psychiatric team within a general hospital offering a consultation service to cover all aspects of psychiatric care in a general hospital setting. A significant part of its work is with overdose, self-injury and other parasuicidal patients. The team that deals with this aspect is multi-disciplinary, comprising nurses, social worker, registrars and trainees of all disciplines. The staff all assess patients and share the same role of 'counsellor'.

The contribution of the separate disciplines within this framework is generally provided through discussion and consultation, but sometimes it is necessary or appropriate to share work with colleagues. The team is organised on the basis that of prime significance is the relationship between the counsellor and the patient, which is principally established at the time of the assessment interview. The assessment worker thus becomes the key worker, and the team should support him or her, rather than compartmentalise and divide between them the patient's problem.

Ann L is 55-years-old and was admitted to the hospital following a severe self-inflicted stabbing with a bread knife. This was her second attempt to kill herself, the first being made thirteen months previously when she took a serious overdose. Because of the need for orthopaedic care at that time, a medical social worker at the orthopaedic hospital became responsible for follow-up action. Ann is married to Tom and has six living children.

The problems following her stabbing were the continuing suicide risk; the fact that she was depressed and interpreted the behaviour of others in a paranoid way; she was very disabled, with rheumatoid arthritis; she felt rejected by her family; she was preoccupied with the state of their house; having recently moved there; she suffered a continued feeling of loss following the death of her 24-year-old son two years previously; and she felt lonely and isolated. A nurse undertook the assessment and highlighted these problems at the daily clinical team meeting with the senior registrar present. We decided that the psychiatric registrar should join the nurse in an interview at the hospital to assess further Ann's mental state and the risk of suicide. Upon discharge, the nurse would continue to be involved and lead the work, but the social worker would also be involved in assessing whether the family would respond to family therapy.

The registrar felt that Ann was suffering from a depressive illness and started appropriate drug therapy. Rather than seeing her paranoid interpretations as part of a set of delusions, he felt that she was simply sensitive to the opinions of others of her and to being in hospital. He made several joint visits with the nurse to assess the value of the antidepressant medicine. This was considerable, and there were great changes in Ann's mood; she was able to take part more actively in family life and other social events.

The nurse visited Ann at home every week for four months to provide emotional support and to focus discussion on the problems the family faced. For most of these the social worker provided advice and support before and after the visits. On five occasions, however, joint visits were arranged, with the social worker concentrating additionally on trying to get the family to agree to joint discussion of various issues, rather than just providing minimal encouragement to individual work with Ann. The difficulties which particularly resulted in this approach were the hostile and indifferent attitudes of the children, of whom there were four in the home aged 16—23, towards their father: the long-standing difficulties in the marital relationship which the couple did not discuss with each other but only separately with the children; the family's feelings about the suicide attempt and subsequent psychiatric treatment; the insecurity for Ann of acknowledging the marital difficulties when she was becoming more reliant on her husband; and the financial problems arising from the husband's tendency to spend most of his wages on gambling or drinking. The family consistently denied the need for family discussion and would not even discuss the possibility, so the social worker joined meetings with the nurse to focus on this issue. There were very fruitful discussions and agreement by some members of the family to join family sessions, but this was not accepted by the husband.

Thus, after going through with Ann and her children the implications of their refusal to discuss things with Tom, the social worker withdrew from direct involvement but continued to provide consultation for the nurse, until the family received a 'notice to quit' and the social worker was again brought in to liaise with the housing department, and act as an advocate on Ann's behalf, arguing on the basis of her disability and emotional vulnerability.

Throughout this period the nurse, social worker and psychiatric registrar discussed the case regularly. They presented it to the Barnes Unit's consultant on two occasions for his opinion. The nurse had formal responsibility for follow-up and communicating with the family's general practitioner. The psychiatric registrar was responsible for the medication. The social work responsibility was for participation in family work, supervision of his nursing colleague in her work in the patient's home, and specific tasks which called for the knowledge and experience of a social worker. Within this allocation of tasks, there was no question of hierarchy, but they were all responsible to the Unit's consultant and, on this basis of equality, related to him.

The nurse continued to see the family at home until seven months after the self-injury. She maintains occasional telephone contact to reinforce the willingness of the Unit to become involved at any time. The final outcome is uncertain. Tom has cleared his debts by using some money from voluntary redundancy, but this is no basis for confidence in the family's long-term ability to meet such basic items as rent and energy. Ann's rheumatoid arthritis, now very severe and crippling, will gradually get worse, while the added problems of ulcerated legs exacerbate the physical difficulties. The medication has proved to be of significant value and has helped Ann to re-establish her life, which is a great improvement over her level of coping in recent years. Tom's refusal to become involved in family discussion, and Ann's refusal to press this, means that there is not much hope for their relationship as the children begin to leave home. Ann is taking her first holiday for ten years to Ireland (where she originated) and the separation and the chance to live for a while with her family of origin may be the final outcome. Or suicide.

Specially written for this book by Nick Welch

*   *   *

In this case study there is very clear task differentiation and role integration, though it is evident that this often varies when the case situation requires a different pattern. There is respect for the professional skills and roles of others and the whole effort is supported by a planned system of consultation, responsibility and opportunities for planning and sharing in a meeting.

Team-training for multi-disciplinary work

There are a variety of proposals to use joint training to promote multi-disciplinary teamwork. Training work teams together was an integral part of the strategy to improve the participation of staff following the 1974 NHS reorganisation (Smith, 1977). Multi-disciplinary groups can improve teamwork by providing joint training in some aspect of the work in which none of them are expert, e.g. a new procedure or administrative structure; or they can be involved in a project where they can work together on some improvement in the service. Another alternative is for each in turn to provide training, and possibly later consultation, in some aspect of their own professional group's work, to others in the team. High-status members of the team should avoid predominating in such activity — lower-status members might initiate proceedings, for example. If necessary, inexperienced trainers can be helped by colleagues from their occupational group from outside the team (for example, a social worker might call on a local social work teacher for a contribution, or a volunteer or the Council of Voluntary Service).

According to Carlaw and Callan (1973), such attempts at team-training are not necessarily sufficient to improve knowledge and skill within professions or focus on the problems of clients, but they do have the advantage of providing an opportunity to 'explore the assumptions and stereotypes they have of each other and of the situation'.

The alternative method of training for teamwork is in the early professional education of each occupational group. There are examples of academic input between professions (e.g. Payne, 1976; Prins, 1973), inter-disciplinary conferences to build mutual acceptance between occupational groups, and increasingly American writers are reporting attempts to join many different kinds of workers together on student placements including students on the equivalent of CSS and CQSW courses (e.g. Austin *et al.*, 1972; Linn *et al.*, 1974).

There is a great deal of literature, including many case studies on multi-disciplinary work, and access to these can be gained by looking at the bibliographies of Lonsdale *et al.* (1980), Marshall *et al.* (1979), Kane (1975) and Tichy (1974). The book by Hall and Hall (1980) about teamwork in a part-time group of social workers is up to date and most useful, and the study by Wise *et al.* (1974) of teamwork in a mental health centre is a seminal work of theory and team-building practice.

The team in its organisational context

The problems of multi-disciplinary teamwork are particularly acute for social workers because they are often vested with responsibility for ensuring that liaison between organisations works (often to the exclusion of doing anything else to make co-operation work) and because they are frequently outposted from their own agencies to others with a different approach, rather than the others joining social work agencies. This puts social workers in the forefront of promoting relationships between organisations, and I have already suggested how important organisational support for teamwork is. It is to this aspect of the relationship between teams and their context that I now turn. Three important relationships are considered: with the host organisation (e.g. managers who are responsible for the team's work), with other teams in the same agency, and with other agencies or parts of them.

The 'host' organisation

The 'host' organisation is a rather inaccurate title for the agency that the team belongs to. Teams' relationships with their hosts are complicated because they share various structures. *Misalignments of structures*, e.g. power, communication, work flow (see pp. 20—1, 66—7), can create problems. For example, conflicts about how the team leader is responsible for shared work (see pp. 13—16) often derive from misalignments in power and responsibility structures.

Structural misalignments can be managed either by representatives of the organisation or by the team, by explaining the problem and, in an enquiry mode, suggesting shared work to find a solution. For example, a team representative might say:

> The team would like communication with other parts of the organisation to be by various different people to spread the workload, to broaden team members' experience and to make sure the team's representative was the most appropriate person. You, on the other hand, seem to prefer the team leader to do all this work. Is there some way of agreeing on the right person in each case?

Obstacles may get in the way of change. Many team members are not well prepared for higher-level meetings, and conventional assumptions about managerial or organisational accountability may make managers doubtful. Many team members who are inexperienced in such meetings behave inappropriately and miss general issues. For example, I was once present at a meeting concerned with the development of an SSD's policy for intermediate treatment, where a representative of one team clearly came with the intention of achieving recognition of a particular project for his team. Having achieved this, he made no further contribution to the meeting, and it later turned out that his team disagreed with some major matter of principle with the policy we agreed, but he did not know enough about the history of discussions or resource and policy questions to contribute. Rehearsal and preparation can get over such problems. Information and views can be shared within the team in a discussion prior to the meeting to help their representative.

Assumptions about accountability can be more difficult to counter. It may be possible to get round this by designated leaders formally delegating colleagues to speak on their behalf. Another important form of preparation is to help the team representatives understand the roles of others they will deal with, and the boundaries of their interests, since it is easy for the uninitiated to upset others unnecessarily by treading on their toes. It will, however, sometimes be necessary to argue that the conventional assumptions should be modified. Spreading the load and staff development can, as I have suggested, be one way of arguing. If the dispute is about who is accountable, a clear understanding that team leaders do not have to direct every activity of the team to be accountable and can accept the management responsibility to *ensure* that work is done properly by having issues discussed in the team meeting is normally acceptable to managers. Sometimes this can be made explicit at the team's meeting. The team leader can say, for instance, 'I think the agency will need to know who is responsible for what in this decision [or case]. Can we make that clear?'

This leads on to the second problem in the team's relationship with the host agency, in that *objectives may differ.* Employees may have legitimate professional aims (e.g. quality of professional service) or personal ones (e.g. advancement), and if they follow them their activities may obstruct or oppose the agency's aims. I have already suggested how teams' aims derive from the needs of the client groups and communities they serve and their ideals and training may conflict with a host organisation's more general policies, so leaders may have to negotiate changes. The inevitability of such conflict can be reduced if the team supplies effective information about its work to change management judgements about the pattern of services.

Other teams

Relationships with other teams present many similar problems, some different ones and some advantages. Teams which have contacts through work may be in conflict for resources or they may be able to ally themselves to achieve something jointly; alliances with managers are far less common. Misalignments of structure and objective can be equally problematic. However, teams of social workers, at least with broadly similar responsibilities, often have similarities of experience and attitudes which allow them to co-operate quite readily.

Other organisations

Co-operation between organisations is very complex, depending on whether the whole organisation, parts of it or individuals are trying to work together, as well as with the extent of the required co-operation. Bleiweiss and Simson (1976), in a study of voluntary and state organisations for the elderly trying to work together, suggest that three different aspects have to be drawn together. There should be similar values, attitudes, decision-making processes, patterns of communication and managerial styles (*organisational integration*), together with similar attitudes to the validity of various professional activities, e.g. social action, caring, the medical role (*professional co-ordination*). Also, the organisations should be secure in their social position, should be strong financially, and have a reasonable amount of certainty about their aims and methods (*environmental adaptation*), otherwise the pattern which other organisations have to relate to is too insecure for stable joint activities to be built up.

Assessing the right way to co-operate

Deciding how to co-operate involves considering, first, what kinds of relationships exist between the organisations, and then what might be desirable. Davidson (1976) proposes the typology of inter-organisational relationships set out in Table 7.1. This applies to all relationships, even with the host agency, since, although there is a power relationship in which more senior managers can direct teams, day-to-day relationships between teams and their managers are like relationships between groups. Very often relationships are at the communication, co-operation and co-ordination levels for all practical purposes. The groups do not actually work together as groups, which is my concern here, but they often behave as though they were representatives of groups.

Table 7.1 *Styles of teamwork between organisations*

Type of relationship	Description
Communication	The organisations merely inform each other of what they are doing
Co-operation	Both organisations are prepared to act to help or support each other
Co-ordination or confederation	Both organisations agree to change their practice activities or boundaries to rationalise their work
Federation	The organisations set up or use a superordinate body to control their joint activities while keeping some independence
Merger	The management of all activities of both organisations is carried out by the same group

Source: adapted from Davidson (1976).

In assessing the desirable form of co-operation, teams could look at the tasks which have to be shared, the level of agreement about objectives and the alignment of various structures in the way already discussed. For example, if two teams in an SSD have to contribute to planning a new service for discharged psychiatric patients, this might be done at a communication level, if it is a matter of putting up ideas to a working party doing the planning. If the teams are dissimilar (e.g. hospital or residential workers and fieldworkers), their structures and objectives are likely to be different and lead to conflict. This will not matter until implementation of the plan is required. At this point, co-operation or co-ordination will be needed, and it is a matter of judgement whether this is better started at the planning stage, or left until after conflicting views are collected and made apparent.

This leads me to consider ways of bringing together different parts of organisations.

Three strategies for joint teamwork

Three useful strategies for dealing with the effects of the problems I have discussed lie in informal relationships, structural relationships and interchanges.

Informal relationships. Relationships between the two groups are different from relationships between individuals who are members of the groups. Both sets of relationships are affected by the setting in which a particular contact takes place: relationships of either kind vary depending on whether they are made mainly in formal meetings or mainly in informal contacts. One way of dealing with difficulties in relationships between a team and elsewhere is, then, to change the setting in which contacts take place, or change the style of contacts. If formal meetings lead to an impasse, one or two representatives meeting informally may be able to resolve something. If individuals are in dispute, a formal contact between larger groups that they represent may sort it out.

Individuals in such situations may be representing their group, or only acting for themselves. If they are representing their group, it is useful for them to consider the extent of their mandate, and freedom of action, and to make this clear to others in advance. We may distinguish: *observers* and *messengers*, who make a contact to gain information and pass it on to their group or to give information on behalf of their group; *delegates*, who are able to interact, but have to conform to objectives and strategies set by their groups; *negotiators*, who can discuss any relevant matters (which may include their objectives), and follow their own strategy, but they have a specified fallback position; and *representatives*, who are able to accept changes in objectives on behalf of their group. There may be limitations to these in any particular contact. If an individual only speaks for himself, it is useful in discussions to draw attention to this and make clear the extent to which other members of his group agree with him. An individual will often say: 'My personal view is this, and I think most people in my group go along with this . . .'; or 'I think I am a bit out of line with my team on this point . . .'

So far I have discussed the ways in which individuals can use their relationships in formal negotiating between teams. Obviously it would be possible to use the individual contacts through work-sharing, as discussed in Chapter 5, to promote relationships which could then be used to encourage co-operation between groups, provided that the individual concerned is happy with and able to make relationships with other organisations or groups. Individuals often have preferences or blind-spots about this. Weirich *et al.* (1977) found in research in the USA that there are a number of different styles of co-operation with other agencies, and it may be useful for teams to identify their members' preferences and use them in contacts accordingly. They identified five kinds of staff whose degree of involvement with outside organisations varied: *isolates* had no contact with outside agencies; *insiders* only had contact with groups which were part of their own agency; *administrators* used formalised channels with outside agencies as well as inside contacts; *bureaucrats* would use other official agencies as well; and *brokers* had a high level of interaction with all kinds of agencies.

Structural relationships. Another way of dealing with relationships between teams is to set up a structure within the organisation to deal with such relationships. I have already looked at many such structures. The link-pin, the matrix and outposting have been dealt with fairly fully. However, such generalised organisational devices may not help to sort out small-scale difficulties, and in any case are complex examples of more basic structures. Such structures fall into eight groups, which are outlined in Table 7.2. There are an infinite number of possibilities in setting up such structures, but they are mainly concerned with defining the amount of effort, the nature of the contact, the amount of shared work, and influence over the other group's work.

Table 7.2 *Structures for co-operation between groups*

Structure	Description
Contact	One or more team members appointed to receive contacts from the other group
Outreach	One or more team members appointed to contact the other group as required
Link	One or more team members appointed to receive contacts or make them at regular intervals
Liaison	One or more team members appointed to have regular links and broad discussions, and to undertake work with members of the other group
Outposting	One or more team members are placed partly or wholly in the other group's setting, and undertakes work with members of this group
Interface	One or more team members are appointed to be equal members of both groups
Interleaving	Team members from both groups take on work in the other
Merger	Both groups undertake all shared work together

Structural relationships are a way of institutionalising and organising contacts between groups so that there need be no anxiety or conflict over what is expected or required, and there is a system for dealing with any problems which arise. When relationship difficulties come up, or new contacts need to be started, the third form of strategy may be helpful.

Interchange. This strategy comprises various ways of getting different groups together to sort out difficulties between them. At the simplest level it may involve more open sharing of documents, plans or exchange of people to spend time with the other group to learn about its structures, styles and aims. If such a programme is organised, clear objectives and commitment from the people involved is required so that they do not get bored or fail to learn from the various activities. If there is an exchange of staff, clear structure and learning objectives are needed with opportunities for feedback so that learners can test out what they have learned, and the receiving group can check that they have picked up the main points of what they were supposed to learn.

More sophisticated exercises involve meetings between the groups to explore difficulties. A number of exercises for this purpose are provided by Dyer (1977, pp. 117—24), Merry and Allerhand (1977, pp. 319—50) and Woodcock (1979). A useful one, commonly used, is to set up a *joint problem-solving work group* to deal with a particular issue that has arisen, and invite members to consider explicitly the process problems they encountered in dealing with the issue, so that the difficulties between the groups can be identified and their working together may help to overcome it. Another alternative is to set up a *joint session* to resolve a problem. The members of each group are invited to list the things which the other groups does that cause problems for them, the things they do that the other group may have problems with, and ways of dealing with the issues. They exchange their lists and discuss them, then have mixed working parties to come up with solutions to the difficulty. Another alternative is the *fishbowl*, which is useful where there are personal jealousies and antipathies which seem to arise from lack of understanding of how the other group works, or the issues it has to face, or where different disciplines or occupational groups are in conflict. Each group in turn simulates a team meeting to resolve an issue of importance to both groups (or invites the other group to an actual team meeting where relevant matters are to be resolved). The other team watches how the team in the fishbowl works, and then reciprocates. Various group meetings, both separate and mixed, can be organised to capitalise on and discuss these experiences. This method may bring interpersonal difficulties to the surface and need a lot of confidence to organise, so an outside consultant may be useful. Various other methods of promoting interchange between the groups can easily be imagined or adapted from the reference books mentioned above.

Breaking off relationships

At times, relationships between groups inside or outside the host agency seem not to be working out, or not worth while, and the question is raised whether contacts should be broken off. Changing priorities, or pressures on time or resources, may also force a change.

One possibility, rather than completely breaking off relationships, is to *reduce involvement*. Where all members of two groups or several representatives meet, for example, contact can be vested in single representatives, provided a system for briefing and informing them of the views of others is also set up. Alternatively, contact can be limited to liaison, rather than regular interchange. Such systems may work better than participants expect simply because there has been closer contact in the past.

When one, some or all sides in a collaboration wish to reduce or break off a contact, however, it is often important to leave the parties feeling good about past contacts and able to deal with any occasional or remaining business which arises. It is therefore useful to have *mutual discussion* about, and preferably agreement on, the change in relationship. It can also be helpful to set up *explicit channels* for starting further contact and *clear boundaries* around what each group will do for the others in future.

Broaching these issues can be difficult, and it is one of the advantages of having a regular review of contacts that breaking off can be raised painlessly. Otherwise, a start can be made by suggesting that 'as we have been meeting some time now, perhaps we could talk over how it's going and any ways we can improve things' — again using the enquiry mode.

Signs which can indicate that a contact might be broken

off are repetition in discussions with no progress (but this might suggest that more effective problem-solving is needed), a lack of topics to discuss, declining and irregular attendance, and a predominance of reports and information-giving rather than negotiation.

8

Practising Teamwork

This chapter is concerned with teamwork in social work practice with clients (individuals, in groups or within their communities). Most of the ideas discussed so far apply to teamwork within the team as an organisational device and also to teamwork in teams formed to work with particular clients or problems. In this final chapter I want to look more closely at the problems of relating teamwork to clients' needs, and co-ordinating the roles of different team members into a service which is relevant for clients.

Casework

Co-ordinating work in individual cases reveals difficulties about over-all objectives as well as co-ordinating different roles and explaining teamwork to the client. Just having agreement to objectives set by one member of the work group is not enough. For them to be shared they should be thrashed out in a meeting with everyone concerned, so that each team member can justify what he or she is doing to the member's own satisfaction, and through this process strengthen commitment to the work group. All team members may also be able to contribute ideas which might not have occurred to one person.

An example of these advantages is the case of an elderly lady, Mrs Jones, living alone, who was not caring for herself adequately. She was reported to the SSD by the local priest and, after assessment, admission to an old people's home was

ruled out because no places were available. Looking for alternatives, the social worker approached the home-help organiser
(HHO), who was unhappy about offering a service because
home helps had not got on well with Mrs Jones in the past.
They decided to call a meeting comprising the social worker,
the HHO, the social work assistant and, as an afterthought,
the priest and the officer-in-charge of a local old people's
home which also provided some day places. At the beginning
of the meeting there was much discussion of the pressure on
places in the home, and the difficulties which the lady presented, but the hidden purpose of this seemed to be to provide
mutual support for putting pressure on the allocation system
for a place in the home than to seek a practical solution to
the problem. This was disputed by the officer-in-charge, who
felt that Mrs Jones would be difficult to deal with if admitted
and impossible to persuade to admit. The discussion was
completely turned about by the priest, who thought that
neighbours had wanted the lady helped to be more sociable
and able to live at home rather than be 'taken away'. This
took the centre of discussion away from the aim of admission
to a home towards finding ways of increasing sociability and
independence. At first the home-help organiser was hostile to
this because she felt that helping Mrs Jones was difficult (and
possibly because the burden would fall on her and her staff).
Closer discussion of the problems narrowed down to Mrs
Jones's increasing arthritis, which led to her inability to keep
the house clean and tidy, and her hostile reactions to others.
All the members of the group felt that dealing with these
might be practicable and discussion moved on to the action
that might be taken.

At this stage some agreement was achieved about objectives
and commitment to them, overcoming the impasse which had
arisen because disputed or unattainable objectives had been
under discussion. In the next part of the meeting, as task
differentiation and role integration are planned, there was
more of an enquiry mode, which meant that people were
encouraged to join in the problem-solving rather than maintain their own position.

Discussion focused first on the arthritis. Two possibilities
were suggested by the social worker and HHO respectively:

introducing aids and adaptations to the house, and involving an occupational therapist (OT) to help Mrs Jones learn new ways of doing her housework. The assistant, a man, pointed out that some jobs around the house were in this area conventionally done by men, and some training in these might be helpful. It was agreed that he could offer this, and that specialists from elsewhere would deal with the other matters. The social worker agreed to contact them, and to provide supervision on his educative role for the assistant. Discussion then turned to Mrs Jones's social contacts. It was possible to arrange attendance at a luncheon club and this might have brought her into contact with old friends again, but several people doubted whether she would agree to this. The priest agreed to get a parishioner to visit her and attend with her to see if this would help. The group then made a list of who had agreed to approach whom about what, when it would be done by, and arranged to report results back to the social worker. The HHO then pointed out that these ideas had not been tested out with Mrs Jones and the agreement was reached that the social worker would visit to discuss with her the various alternatives which the team had considered and see what plan she would agree to. He wrote a variety of different possibilities on sheets, showing which staff and volunteers would be involved in each programme, and she eventually selected one of these, which excluded the luncheon-club idea. She agreed, however, to accept a mid-day meal delivered to her home, and it was arranged that another lady nearby who also received this meal would join her in her home.

In the latter part of the meeting the various team members were actively involved in planning, and this led to several well-integrated contributions to helping Mrs Jones. The plans and who was to be involved in different roles were explicitly discussed with her, and the various tasks of different team members were defined and planned. A co-ordinator of the arrangements was designated to ensure that things worked out satisfactorily.

In this planning meeting there was also an attempt to identify specific tasks and skills, arrange them in a sequence and then plan how to work in the simultaneous task relationships. The non-professionals (assistant, priest) made useful

contributions based on their particular skills and local knowledge.

Groupwork

The issues raised by groupwork in teams are twofold. First, as
Whitaker (1975) shows, the support of members around those
doing groupwork is essential in enabling a group to start at all.
Then there are special problems for people sharing responsibility for a group: they become a group within a group, the
client group relates both to the groupworker's group (if there
is more than one staff member), through them, and in other
ways to the team, and to the individuals within it. Complex
relationships arise and cause difficulties. The following two
examples demonstrate some of these issues.

A young probation officer joined a team and found that
his caseload contained two offenders who had been put on
probation for violent offences. He thought of starting a group
for violent offenders and approached his senior, who agreed
and supported him. Plans were made to set up the group.
Obviously additional group members would be needed and
the probation officer approached colleagues in the team.
Although several had relevant clients and supported the idea
of the group, they did not in fact refer any, and the whole
project collapsed. The probation officer and senior expressed
a certain amount of grievance about this at a team meeting.
Other team members felt that they had not been consulted
about the idea except in very general terms and had felt unhappy about referring their clients to another colleague,
because they were not sure what effects his activities in the
group would have on their work with the clients, and they
did not know his approach well enough to trust him.

This team (typical of many in the probation and after-
care service) was leader-centred and individualistic in style;
the workers were responsible for their own cases, and communication and planning was mediated through the senior.
This structure disguised the fact that the hopeful groupworker
had not achieved legitimacy from the team as a whole, but
only from the senior, who was not in a position to deliver the

support of others for a groupwork project (although the structure served well for casework consultation).

The problems might have been reduced with individual negotiations about task differentiation with each client's officer and joint discussions about the purposes and running of the group in which the whole team could have joined the planning. The leader-centred, individualistic style of the team need not have been totally supplanted, but in this instance wide consultation and collaborative planning were needed.

The second case example also concerns a probation officer in which three officers ran a group for adolescents who had committed serious motoring offences. The three officers had set the group up with the agreement of the rest of the team. One of the officers had experience of automobile engineering and the plan was to have activities based on learning about cars, around which there would be opportunities for more personal discussion. A number of problems arose. First, the amount of time involved in planning and running the group, getting vehicles to work on, and finance for or loans of small items of equipment turned out to be considerable. Second, there was pressure from the group for greater involvement, and rather than a weekly group it was developing into a day workshop for unemployed youngsters. Third, this led away from the mainly therapeutic plan towards a project for finding work in the same area for some of the offenders. This led to criticism from other members of the team that a disproportionate amount of time and activity was being spent on the group by the staff involved, and others were therefore having to carry a heavier workload. The three officers involved felt that they had made a lot of progress with the group both as a group and as individuals. Many members of the group valued it and felt it was the first project they had experienced to help them on their own terms. They in turn felt that the critical officers were jealous of their successful colleagues ('They've never done any good and they don't want to see this succeed either') and urged their group leaders to continue the development of the group.

There are many aspects to this situation. It shows how a group project, initially well supported within a team, can run into difficulties because the group and the staff allied with it take on the position of an autonomous group, even though they remain within the team. The distance from the team created by the strength of the group then easily harms the success of the team as a group.

Residential and day care

I do not propose to discuss residential and day care at length because a companion book in this series by Roger Clough contains a discussion of teamwork relevant to these settings. This section merely points to some important issues which distinguish teamwork in residential and day-care settings from fieldwork and to those opportunities for improving teamwork discussed in this book which particularly apply to this field.

Perhaps the most obvious factor is that residential and day-care teams spend substantial periods of time with groups of children. This makes it difficult to plan separate periods of work with clients as field workers can. Moreover, part of the treatment is considered to be the total milieu within which the client lives. This means that rather than being carried out in the client's home or the social worker's office, residential and day-care work rely on the separation of the client from the normal social milieux and relationships, so social workers have to substitute for those relationships and provide thera- peutic treatment (i.e. that designed to change some aspect of the client's life for the better). In many instances staff and clients are sharing responsibility for the activities and the milieu in which they work together, while it is also the responsibility of the staff to manage the institution on behalf of the agency. This dual responsibility to different groups provokes severe problems for social workers in this position, perhaps most clearly set out by the workers of the Harlesden Community Project (1979, pp. 294–318). In this project an attempt to share responsibility among staff appeared to con- flict with the agency's needs for having hierarchical control within the team that could connect with their own structure. Further sharing with residents made this worse. Part of the problem for workers in this project may have been that they were not prepared to accept a semi-hierarchical link-pin approach but wanted equal access for relevant workers throughout the hierarchy (1979, pp. 198—9).

Another issue is the extent to which residents are part of the team, and are responsible for the management of the milieu as well. This is an important part of working in therapeutic communities advocated by writers such as Jones (1968) and Wills (1971). There are examples of conversion from conventional to 'shared' responsibility (Hague, 1976; Grieve, 1968; Wills, 1971) even in local authority homes, which have to fit into a hierarchical system.

To sum up the extra difficulties of teamwork in residential and day-care, then, the problems of long-term personal contact rather than short-term treatment contact as in the field mean that teamwork has to be directly based on mutual support and personal trust. In the field careful planning prior to contact with clients can reduce the need for this. Rather than use collaborative teamwork, however, many residential and day-care settings deal with this issue by having strict hierarchies and boundaries to reduce the stress. This solution to the problem may be encouraged by the perhaps unjustified assumption that poorly trained staff of low status ought not to be joined in treatment responsibility, though, as I said when discussing non-professionals (pp. 93—4), if they are, then substantial improvement in the quality of service to residents often results. Another point is that the boundaries of sharing with clients, and task and role clarification, once worked out can help to relate a shared responsibility system to a conventional hierarchical structure in the agency.

Community work

The issues for community workers in deciding where the boundary lies (if anywhere) between the professional team and the public being served are just as difficult as in residential and day-care. These, together with the problems of creating teamwork in a complex, often changing situation, are demonstrated in the following case example.

A family advice centre was set up on a deprived council estate with the aim, not only of providing a personal advice service relevant to the people living there, but also of promoting a tenants' group and other mutual help groups. Although the centre was starting from a welfare base, it was hoped that it would be able to expand to form the core of a community centre with wider interests. Eventually a number of volunteer advisers were recruited to provide service in the advice centre, and they formed a group which provided representatives to the management group of the centre, which comprised some local authority officials and three representatives of local organisations, one of whom was also a local councillor. At the same time, funding for the centre as an offshoot of the social services department was altered so that it became in effect an autonomous organisation employing the advice centre worker, a secretary and a newly employed community worker. Two months later a further worker was appointed, and she was one of the volunteers who had been a representative on the committee. Unable any longer to represent the volunteers on the committee she resigned, and was replaced by another volunteer.

A staff group was thus formed, to be added to a clear management group and the volunteer group. As the community worker continued his activities, a number of street-level groups built around mothers caring for pre-school children were set up, as well as a support committee deriving primarily from a local sports and social club, and principally concerned with fund-raising. An issue subsequently arose when a member of that committee working with the former volunteer who was now an employee of the centre formed a personal relationship which led to the break-up of the committee member's marriage. His wife subsequently sought help from the advice centre, which gave help whose results the committee member disliked. He made complaints to the management committee of the centre suggesting that the activities of the advice centre were questionable. A full-scale (but rather confidential) row ensued.

In this situation no one had behaved unreasonably, or in any way which would have caused comment if the various parties had not been both personally involved in the community, professionally involved in work at the centre, and indirectly in various management and work relationships. In dealing with this the staff and management groups had a number of advantages. First, within the staff group a pattern of mutually supportive relationships had been worked out, the advice given and its possible ramifications had been openly discussed, and then the advice centre worker had privately talked over the position with the worker/former volunteer. She was then able to influence her friend to understand the role of the advice centre more positively. This example of the open discussion and sharing of work between the volunteers and professionals and the mutual support available shows how this can help deal with difficult situations. The way in which the personal relationship problems were dealt with reflects the sort of approach discussed in Chapter 5. The other helpful way in which the issue was dealt with was in the careful separation of the roles of the staff group from the responsibility of the management group. Following the professional advice tendered by the staff group the management group considered the matter independently by appointing a sub-committee which excluded the volunteer representatives, but included the councillor, people from the community and one of the local authority representatives; the sub-committee then heard evidence from representatives of the staff group and the volunteers. In this way each group with an interest was represented, but conflicts of interest were avoided.

In this case, then, a clear understanding of roles and a well-understood structure were combined with a concern for people and for making sure that justice was seen to be done, in order to deal with some of the uncertainties and blurring of boundaries which often arise in community work.

Conclusion

Teamwork is a way of organising work and managing the people who do it. It is concerned with planning how to work together in general and in particular cases. It offers opportunities for crossing the conventional boundaries between different kinds of work and different agencies. It is several different ways of promoting a more planned, organised, accountable and satisfying way of providing social services which can be more efficient, more relevant to and involving of clients, and effective in defining and achieving the aims which social services agencies set out to meet.

But it provides opportunities and possibilities to mould to the individuals who would work together rather than a set pattern which is the answer to all their problems. And it presents serious problems and policy issues which social services teamworkers should take into account in their work.

I hope this book helps them see and grasp the possibilities, while offering a start towards dealing with the problems of teamwork. ⟩

Abbreviations

BASW	British Association of Social Workers
CQSW	Certificate of Qualification in Social Work
CSS	Certificate in Social Service
DHSS	Department of Health and Social Security
EWO	Education Welfare Officer
NASW	National Association of Social Workers (USA)
NHS	National Health Service
OPS	Operational Priority Scheme
OT	Occupational Therapist
SSDs	Social Services Departments

References

This list of works referred to in the text covers a few of the more important and accessible writings about teamwork but is by no means comprehensive, and particularly excludes the field of education. The reason for this is the need to keep the present work as a *practice* text, and I have avoided giving chapter and verse for every statement. However, through the works mentioned here, it is possible to obtain access to much of the literature, and I have marked useful introductory texts with an asterisk *, texts containing practical team-building exercises with a dagger †, and works containing surveys of useful background material or which are particularly influential with a double-dagger ‡.

Ager, G. (1979) 'Aides for the elderly during inclement times', *Health and Social Service Journal*, 89(4648), pp. 806—7.
Anderson, R. E. and Carter, I. E. (1974) *Human Behavior in the Social Environment*, Chicago, Aldine.
Ash, E., Barr, H., Cornwell, A., Ruddick, J. and Skidmore, A. (1980) *The Certificate in Social Service: A Progress Report to the Council from the Staff*, CCETSW Paper 9:4.
*Austin, M. J. (1978) *Professionals and Paraprofessionals*, New York, Human Sciences Press.
Austin, M. J., Kelleher, E. and Smith, P. L. (eds) (1972) *The Field Consortium: Manpower Development and Training in Social Welfare and Corrections*, Tallahassee, Florida, State University System of Florida.
Baker, R. (1976a) 'The multirole practitioner in the generic orientation to social work practice', *British Journal of Social Work*, 6(3), pp. 327—52.
Baker, R. (1976b) *The Interpersonal Process in Generic Social Work: An Introduction*, Bundoora, Australia, Preston Institute of Technology Press, Occasional Papers in Social Work No. 2.
*Barker, R. L. and Briggs, T. L. (1969) *Using TEAMS to Deliver Social Services*, New York, Division of Continuing Education and Manpower Development, Syracuse University School of Social Work, Manpower Monograph No. 1.

BASW (1977) *The Social Work Task*, Birmingham, BASW Publications.

Bleiweiss, L. and Simson, S. (1976) 'Building a comprehensive geriatric health care system: a case study', *Journal of Community Health*, 2(2), pp. 144—52.

†Brandes, D. and Phillips, H. (1979) *Gamesters' Handbook: 140 Games for Teachers and Group Leaders*, London, Hutchinson.

*Brieland, D., Briggs, T. and Leuenberger, P. (eds) (1973) *The Team Model of Social Work Practice*, New York, Syracuse University School of Social Work, Manpower Monograph No. 5.

Briggs, T. (1973) 'Identifying team functional roles and specialisation', in Brieland *et al.* (1973).

*Brill, N. I. (1976) *Teamwork: Working Together in the Human Services*, Philadelphia, J. B. Lippincott.

Bush, S. (1980) 'Keeping your team on target', *Community Care*, 20 March, pp. 20—1.

Carlaw, R. W. and Callan, L. B. (1973) 'Team training: an experiment with promise', *Health Service Reports*, 88(4), pp. 328—36.

Cockerill, E. (1953) 'The interdependence of the professions in helping people', *Social Casework*, 34(9), pp. 371—8.

Community Care (1980) 'Unemployed get the chance to be social workers', *Community Care* 17 July, p. 8.

Corney, R. and Briscoe, M. (1977) 'Investigation into two different types of attachment schemes', *Social Work Today*, 9(15), pp. 10—14.

†Crosby, R. P. (1972) *Planning Recommendations or Action: A Team-Development Guidebook*, La Jolla, California, University Associates (pamphlet).

Davidson, S. M. (1976) 'Planning and co-ordination of social services in multi-organisational contexts', *Social Service Review*, 50(1), pp. 117—37.

Day, P., Rhodes, V. and Truefitt, T. (1978) 'Priorities and an area team', *Social Work Today*, 10(7), pp. 22—3.

‡DHSS (1978) *Social Service Teams: the Practitioners' Viewpoint*, London, HMSO.

Dingwall, R. (1980) 'Problems of teamwork in primary care', in Lonsdale *et al.* (1980).

*†Dyer, W. G. (1977) *Team Building: Issues and Alternatives*, Reading, Mass., Addison-Wesley.

Ends, E. J. and Page, C. W. (1977) *Organizational Team Building*, Cambridge, Mass., Winthrop Publishers Inc.

Etzioni, A. (1975) *A Comparative Analysis of Complex Organisations: On Power, Involvement, and their Correlates*, New York, Free Press.

Fiedler, F. E. (1965) 'Leadership — a new model', in Gibb (1969).

Filley, A. C. (1975) *Interpersonal Conflict Resolution*, Glenview, Ill., Scott, Foresman & Co.

Fine, S. A. and Wiley, W. W. (1971) *An Introduction to Functional Task Analysis: A Scaling of Selected Tasks from the Social Welfare Field*, Kalamazoo, Mich., W. E. Upjohn Institute for Employment Research.

Fraser, C. (1978a) 'Communication', in Tajfel and Fraser (1978).
Fraser, C. (1978b) 'Small groups: I and II', in Tajfel and Fraser (1978).
French, J. R. P. and Raven, B. H. (1959) 'The bases of social power', in D. Cartwright and A. Zander (eds), *Group Dynamics: Theory and Research*, 3rd edn, London, Tavistock, 1974.
Gartner, A. (1971) *Paraprofessionals and their Performance: A survey of Education, Health and Social Service Programmes*, New York, Praeger.
‡Gibb, C. A. (ed.) (1969) *Leadership: Selected Readings*, Harmondsworth, Penguin.
Gostick, C. (1976) 'Work flow in an area team: preliminary analysis. Part 1: general trends', *Clearing House for Local Authority Social Services Research*, 1976(10), pp. 1–36.
Goulstone, R. and Jones, E. (1976) 'General practitioner–social services liaison: case studies of two schemes in South Dorest', *Clearing House for Local Authority Social Services Research*, 7, pp. 95–115.
Grieve, J. (1968) 'Some experiences in shared responsibility with normal and abnormal adolescents', in A. T. Barron (ed.), *Studies in Environment Therapy, Vol. 1*, Planned Environment Therapy Trust, Worth, Sussex, pp. 83–91.
Grosser, C. F., Henry, W. E. and Kelly, J. G. (1969) *Nonprofessionals in the Human Services*, San Francisco, Jossey-Bass.
Hadley, R. and McGrath, M. (1979) 'Patch-based social services', *Community Care*, 11 October, pp. 16–18.
Hague, G. (1976) 'Struggling to build a shared responsibility system', *Residential Social Work*, 16(8), pp. 207–13.
Hall, A. (1975a) *A Point of Entry*, London, Allen & Unwin.
Hall, A. (1975b) 'Policymaking: more judgement than luck', *Community Care*, 6 August, pp. 16–18.
Hall, A. and Hall, P. (1980) *Part-Time Social Work*, London, Heinemann.
Harlesden Community Project Workers (1979) *Community Work and Caring for Children: A Community Project in an Inner City Local Authority*, Ilkley, Owen Wells.
Hey, A. (1979) 'Organising teams – alternative patterns', in Marshall *et al.* (1979).
Hiltner, S. (1958) 'Tension and mutual support among the helping professions', *Social Service Review*, 31(4), pp. 377–89.
Horwitz, J. J. (1970) *Team Practice and the Specialist*, Springfield, Ill., Charles C. Thomas.
Hunt, M. (1979) 'Possibilities and problems of interdisciplinary teamwork', in Marshall *et al.* (1979).
Jeans, M. S. (1978) *Role Analysis in Field Social Work: The Development of a New Model*, Devon Social Services Department.
Jones, M. (1968) *Social Psychiatry in Practice: The Idea of the Therapeutic Community*, Harmondsworth, Penguin.
Kane, R. A. (1975) *Training for Teamwork: With an Annotated Bibliography of Teaching Materials*, New York: Syracuse University School of Social Work, Manpower Monograph No. 5.

Kane, R. A. (1980) 'Multi-disciplinary teamwork in the United States: trends, issues, and implications for the social worker', in Lonsdale *et al.* (1980).

Lamberts, H. and Riphagen, F. E. (1975) 'Working together in a team for primary health care — a guide to dangerous country', *Journal of the Royal College of General Practitioners*, 25, pp. 745—52.

Lawrence, P. R. and Lorsch, J. W. (1967) *Organization and Environment: Managing Differentiation and Integration*, Homewood, Ill., Irwin.

Lewis, J. W. (1975) 'Management team development: will it work for you?', *Personnel*, 52 (July—August), pp. 11—25.

Likert, R. (1961) *New Patterns of Management*, New York, McGraw-Hill.

Linn, M. W., Stein, S., Carter, J. S. and Linn, B. S. (1974) 'The CARE Project: interdisciplinary and community-oriented approach to training social work students', *Journal of Education for Social Work*, 10(2), pp. 47—50.

*Lonsdale, S., Webb, A. and Briggs, T. L. (eds) (1980) *Teamwork in the Personal Social Services and Health Care: British and American Perspectives*, London, Croom Helm.

Lukes, S. (1974) *Power: a Radical View*, London, Macmillan.

McIntosh, J. and Dingwall, R. (1978) 'Teamwork in theory and practice', in R. Dingwall and J. McIntosh (eds), *Readings in the Sociology of Nursing*, London, Churchill Livingstone.

Marshall, M., Preston-Shoot, M. and Wincott, E. (1979) *Teamwork: For and Against*, Birmingham, BASW Publications.

†Merry, U. and Allerhand, M. E. (1977) *Developing Teams and Organizations*, Reading, Mass., Addison-Wesley.

Odhner, F. (1970) 'Group dynamics of the interdisciplinary team', *American Journal of Occupational Therapy*, 24(7), pp. 484—7.

Parsloe, P. (1972) 'Why don't probation officers run client groups?', *Probation*, 18(1), pp. 4—8.

Parsloe, P. (1978) 'Some educational implications', in DHSS (1978).

Parsloe, P. (1981) *Social Services Area Teams*, London, Allen & Unwin.

Pavalko, R. M. (1971) *Sociology of Occupations and Professions*, Itasca, Ill., F. E. Peacock.

Payne, L. (1976) 'Interdisciplinary experiment', *Social Work Today*, 6(22), pp. 691—3.

Payne, M. (1977) 'Dusting up on community care', *Community Care*, 6 July, pp. 16—17.

Payne, M. (1979) *Power, Authority and Responsibility in Social Services: Social Work in Area Teams*, London, Macmillan.

Payne, M. (1980) 'A self-positioning exercise in a social work course', *Social Work Education Reporter*, 28(2), pp. 10—14.

Payne, M. (1981) 'Staff development in the team', in J. R. Cypher (ed.), *The Task of the Team Leader*, Birmingham, BASW Publications.

Perry, R. (1979) 'Taking risks with children', *Community Care*, 4 January, pp. 23—4.

Priestley, P., McGuire, J., Flegg, D., Hemsley, V. and Welham, D. (1978) *Social Skills and Problem-Solving: A Handbook of Methods,* London, Tavistock.

Prins, H. A. (1973) 'Medical education: the social worker's contribution', *Social Work Today,* 4(4), pp. 119—27.

‡Ribeaux, P. and Poppleton, S. E. (1978) *Psychology and Work: An Introduction,* London, Macmillan.

Riessman, F. and Popper, H. (1968) *Up From Poverty: New Careers Ladders for Nonprofessionals,* New York, Harper & Row.

Rubin, I. M. and Beckhard, R. (1972) 'Factors influencing the effectiveness of health teams', *Milbank Memorial Fund Quarterly,* 50(3), pp. 317—35.

Schwartz, E. E. and Sample, W. C. (1972) *The Midway Office: An Experiment in the Organization of Work Groups,* New York, NASW.

Shaw, M. E. (1964) 'Communication networks', in L. Berkowitz (ed.), *Advances in Experimental Social Psychology, Vol. 1,* New York, Academic Press.

Sheps, C. G. (1974) 'Developmental perspectives on interprofessional education', in H. Rehr (ed.), *Medicine and Social Work: An Exploration in Interprofessionalism,* New York, Prodist.

Smith, D. (1977) 'Team and management-led training', *Health and Social Service Journal,* 87(4560), pp. F5—8.

Stogdill, R. M. (1948) 'Personal factors associated with leadership', in Gibb (1969).

Tajfel, H. (1978) 'Intergroup behaviour', in Tajfel and Fraser (1978).

Tajfel, H. and Fraser, C. (eds) (1978) *Introducing Social Psychology,* Harmondsworth, Penguin.

Teare, R. J. (1970) 'Background and rationale for the symposium', in Teare and McPheeters (1970).

Teare, R. J. and McPheeters, H. L. (1970) *Manpower Utilization in Social Welfare: A Report based on a Symposium on Manpower Utilization in Social Welfare Services,* Atlanta, Georgia, Social Welfare Manpower Project, Southern Regional Education Board.

Thigpen, J. D. (1979) 'Perceptional differences in the supervision of paraprofessional mental health workers', *Community Mental Health Journal,* 15(2), pp. 139—48.

Thomas, D. N. and Warburton, R. W. (1977) *Community Work in a Social Services Department: A Case Study,* London, National Institute for Social Work and Personal Social Services Council.

Tichy, M. K. (1974) *Health Care Teams: An Annotated Bibliography,* New York, Praeger.

Tuckman, B. W. (1965) 'Developmental sequence in small groups', *Psychological Bulletin,* 63(6), pp. 384—99.

Vroom, V. H. and Yetton, P. W. (1973) *Leadership and Decision-Making,* University of Pittsburgh Press.

Walton, R. E. (1969) *Interpersonal Peacemaking: Confrontation and Third Party Consultation,* Reading, Mass., Addison-Wesley.

Webb, A. L. (1975) 'Co-ordination between health and personal social services: a question of quality', European Seminar on the Interaction of Social Welfare and Health Personnel in the Delivery of Services, Vienna.

Webb, A. L. and Hobdell, M. (1980) 'Co-ordination and teamwork in the health and personal social services', in Lonsdale *et al.* (1980).

Weirich, T. W., Perlmutter, F. D. and Richan, W. C. (1977) 'Inter-organizational behavior patterns of line staff and services integration', *Social Service Review*, 51(4), pp. 674–89.

Whitaker, D. S. (1975) 'Some conditions for effective work with groups', *British Journal of Social Work*, 5(4), pp. 423–39.

Wicks, R. J. (1978) *Human Services: New Careers and Roles in the Helping Professions*, Springfield, Ill., Charles C. Thomas.

Wills, W. D. (1971) *Spare the Child*, Harmondsworth, Penguin.

‡Wise, H., Beckhard, R., Rubin, I. and Kyte, A. L. (1974) *Making Health Teams Work*, Cambridge, Mass., Ballinger Publishing Co.

Wood, W. T. (1978) 'Blueprint for developing probation teams', *Federal Probation*, 42(2), pp. 15–17.

*†Woodcock, M. (1979) *Team Development Manual*, Farnborough, Gower Press.

Wright, J. (1978) 'The practice . . . and perfection', *Health and Social Service Journal*, 88(4612), pp. 1160–2.

Index